The
Psychic
Mafia

By Allen Spraggett
New Worlds Of the Unexplained
The Case For Immortality
The World of the Unexplained
Kathryn Kuhlman: The Woman Who Believes in Miracles
Probing The Unexplained
The Bishop Pike Story
The Unexplained

By Allen Spraggett with William V. Rauscher
Arthur Ford: The Man Who Talked With the Dead

By William Rauscher with Allen Spraggett
The Spiritual Frontier

The
Psychic
Mafia

M. Lamar Keene
as told to Allen Spraggett
FoMewords by Ray Hyman and William V. Rauscher

Prometheus Books

59 John Glenn Drive
Amherst, NewYork 14228-2197

Published 1997 by Prometheus Books

01 00 99 98 97   5 4 3 2 1

Library of Congress Cataloging-in-Publication Data

Keene, M. Lamar.
    The psychic mafia / M. Lamar Keene ; as told to Allen Spraggett ;
forewords by Ray Hyman and William V. Rauscher.
        p.   cm.
    Originally published: New York : St. Martin's Press, 1976.
    Includes bibliographical references (p.   ).
    ISBN 1–57392–161–0 (pbk. : alk. paper)
    1. Spiritualism—Controversial literature. I. Spraggett, Allen.
II. Title.
BF1042.K28   1997
133.9′1′092—dc21
[B]   97–25291
                                                                  CIP

Printed in Canada on acid-free paper

FOR MY ADOPTIVE MOTHER,
FLORENCE HUTCHISON:

*Who knew the worst
but believed the best*

AND TO MY NATURAL PARENTS,
MORRIS AND LUCILLE KEENE:

*Who taught me the difference
between right and wrong in
the beginning.*

In this book some proper names have been changed to protect not the guilty but the innocent.

I, Lamar Keene, hereby affirm and warrant that the experiences related in this book, written in collaboration with Allen Spraggett and William Rauscher, are the truth and nothing but the truth (though, it should be added, not necessarily the whole truth, which would be even worse). These experiences are from my career of thirteen years as a fraudulent spiritualist medium.

Lamar Keene

CONTENTS

FOREWORD

Ray Hyman

M. Lamar Keene's *Psychic Mafia* brings to mind an incident that occurred when I was a teenager. I was attending a spiritualist message reading service. The guest speaker had each of us write our name and a question on a piece of paper and then fold the paper. An usher collected the folded messages in a basket which she then placed beside the speaker's lectern. The speaker, who had been blindfolded, would reach into the basket, pull out a folded message, and hold it to his forehead. After a dramatic pause he would call out someone's name. The named person would then stand and the speaker would provide an answer to the question. Presumably this answer was supplied by the spirits. The questioner would acknowledge that the answer was indeed appropriate for the question she had written. The speaker would then take another message from the basket, call out a name, and provide an appropriate answer.

What I have described in the preceding paragraph is

the way the message reading was supposed to take place. On this occasion, however, the speaker was having obvious difficulties. He was getting along in years and his eyesight was not very good. He was having trouble getting his secret peek at the message before he placed the folded paper to his forehead. So he pulled his blindfold away from his eyes with one hand while he blatantly opened the message with the other. After he read its contents, he refolded it, pulled his blindfold back in place, and continued with his routine.

I looked at the members of the audience to see how they would react to this obvious display of cheating. The audience consisted mostly of elderly women and a few elderly men. I was the only young person. To my surprise, not one of them was looking at the speaker. Some were gazing at the ceiling, some were staring into their laps, and others had their eyes closed. The woman sitting next to me was one of those looking at the ceiling. I nudged her and pointed to the speaker at the moment he was opening a message. She looked at me instead. I whispered for her to look at the speaker. She turned and looked at the back of the room and then turned back to me. I kept urging her to look at the speaker. She leaned back and resumed staring at the ceiling.

This bizarre behavior by the audience both puzzled and amazed me. Only after I thought about it some more did it dawn on me what was going on. These people did not want to see the speaker cheating! They wanted to believe that he was providing them communications from their departed loved ones. This belief was an obvious source of comfort to them, so important, in fact, that they would go to any lengths to avoid having it challenged. They dealt with this conspicuous example of cheating by simply not looking. These people, desperately grieving for their loved ones, had found hope and joy in the promise of reestablishing contact. This belief, once established, was too precious to expose to the possibility of refutation. The members of the audience had created for themselves a self-sealing belief system—no matter what external events threatened to puncture their belief, they were always ready to seal the puncture and keep the system intact.

Keene and his partner were far more sophisticated deceivers than the bungling message reader I have recalled. Keene apparently put on dazzling displays of materializations, trumpet séances, apports, billet reading, and other feats attributed to spirit agency. Keene details the many ways he obtained specific information on his sitters. He provided them convincing reasons to believe what they most wanted to believe. Not just the members of his congregation would like to believe in communication with the dead and survival after death. Most everyone would love to know that spiritual survival is true and that we can contact those who have already passed into that state. Keene and his partner provided the excuse for their clients to shed doubt and embrace without reservation the "truths" of spiritualism.

As you read this important exposé, you should resist the temptation to dismiss those who have been duped by mediumistic trickery as gullible. The Stanford psychologist Phil Zimbardo has labeled this tendency as *The "Not Me" Syndrome.*[1] Zimbardo and his coauthors also refer to this as *The Illusion of Personal Invulnerability.* They view this illusion as "a barrier to more effective control over our own attitudes and actions. . . ." They go on to say:

---

1. P. G. Zimbardo, E. B. Ebbesen, and C. Maslach, *Influencing Attitudes and Changing Behavior,* 2d ed. (Reading, Mass.: Addison-Wesley, 1977).

Such an orientation is dangerous because it alienates us from the human condition. By setting ourselves apart from others, we do not learn the important message from their experience—namely, that the source of their suffering, loss of face, or fall from grace may lie not in their personal weaknesses nor in the stars, but in *the power of the situation.*[2]

We can gain many things from reading this book. We can learn the variety of ways in which mediums create their dramatic effects. We discover the sometimes subtle and sometimes obvious ways that they gain "evidential" information about their sitters. The most important lesson I think you will learn, however, is not to fall prey to the "Not Me" Syndrome. The key is not that a small group of people were taken in by Keene and his partner. Rather, it is that *all* of us can be deceived given the right circumstances. Maybe you would not have been fooled by Keene's trumpet séance. But if you have never attended one, how can you be sure? Perhaps, even if you were deeply grieving over the loss of a loved one, and you had no idea how Keene was producing his phenomena without spiritual agency, you still would resist the temptation to succumb to his message. But can you be sure? Perhaps under no circumstances would you believe that someone was actually talking to the dead. As a psychologist, however, I have little doubt that circumstances can be arranged such that you would be susceptible to deception.

So what should we learn from this remarkable book? My claim is that we are much more similar to one another than we like to admit. Those people who willingly gave their money to Keene have basically the same sorts of brains and cultural heritage that we all share. They are not

---

2. Ibid., p. 3.

a separate species who possess a gullibility gene. One thing that makes them susceptible to the wiles of Keene and his fellow mediums is their deep sense of loss from the death of an important person in their lives. Others, of course, may feel such loss and still not succumb to the medium's ploys. Is this because they just happened not to have encountered the mediums? Or have they acquired immunity through other means? These are important questions. They suggest that we do not get very far by simply dividing the world into the gullible and the not-gullible. We will begin to make progress when we refocus the questions to ask what factors and circumstances can lead any one of us to succumb to or to resist the attempts of people and forces out in the world that are trying to control us.

FOREWORD

The Rev. Canon William V. Rauscher

This book is true.

At first, when I met Lamar Keene, the former fraudulent medium whose story it is, I found his revelations in some respects almost incredible.

Oh, I knew, as does every serious investigator of the psychic scene (and I have been one for more than eighteen years) that fraud existed. There was the exposé at Camp Chesterfield in 1960 (described in this book) when infrared film of a materialization séance showed that the "spirits" were staff mediums dressed up in chiffon ectoplasm. I had personally checked out Camp Silver Belle, a spiritualist establishment in Ephrata, Pennsylvania, and Camp Chesterfield, and found rampant fraud. And I had heard of other cases, other exposures.

But with all the whispers, rumors, and suspicions nobody really knew how widespread the fraud was, whether it was organized or haphazard, or whether spiritualist authorities actively connived in it or merely winked at it. What was needed to set us straight was the inside story from someone who knew. And who would know? Only one who had been part of the fraud.

We now have that story—in this book.

Lamar Keene's account is supported by a wealth of documentary evidence, which I have examined. I have met and talked with some of those he duped while he was a medium. I have checked out the church of which he formerly was minister-medium. His story is fact, not fiction.

In my judgment, this book may be one of the most significant in the recent history of psychical research. It will not be so important for the professional parapsychologist (who no doubt will tend to feel that Lamar's tricks wouldn't have fooled him) as for the interested layman, the average person who shares today's popular fascination with anything psychic.

The enormous rise of interest in psychic phenomena and ESP in the last ten years has made it easier for the fake medium and clairvoyant to gain clients. A recent poll showed that a majority of Americans now believe in such phenomena. This new climate of opinion is a gold mine for the phony psychic.

The general public, softened up by watching mentalists on television and reading in popular magazines about psychic experiments in labs and universities, is prone to overbelief. The average person is exceedingly easy to fool. No book could ever detail all the methods by which the fake psychic or medium performs his wonders. Most people, with no inkling of such methods, believe in psychic phenomena much too readily.

This may sound strange coming from one who accepts the reality of paranormal manifestations (as attested in my own book, *The Spiritual Frontier*, an account of my psychic explorations). However, I have spent as much time arguing some people out of an overly credulous attitude toward the subject as arguing others into being open-minded toward it.

As Lamar's story devastatingly reveals, the greatest friend the fraudulent medium has is *overbelief* on the part of his victims. Lamar calls it "the true believer syndrome." The need to believe in phony wonders sometimes exceeds not only logic but, seemingly, even sanity.

A portrayal of this very attitude can be found in the unusual opera, *The Medium*, by Gian-Carlo Menotti. The central character is a fake medium, Madame Flora, who one day tells her sitters that all the wonderful phenomena she has produced were fraudulent. And the result of this confession? The sitters refuse to believe her!

Madame Flora says:

> Listen to me!
> There never was a séance!
> I cheated you!
> Do you understand?
> Cheated you, cheated you!

But the true believers won't give up their deluded faith. Echoes of this are found in Lamar's story and are for me perhaps the most terrifying part.

In my pastoral ministry, as a priest with a profound belief in the importance of psychic experience for religion, I quickly learned how vulnerable the bereaved are to any promise of reassurance that their beloved dead still live. People who have lost one they cherished will travel anywhere, pay anything, *believe anything*, it seems, to hear again that voice that is stilled. I'm personally besieged with requests to recommend "a good medium."

Now, I believe that "good mediums" exist. I believe I have met some of them. Not all mediums are dishonest, and this book is not intended to discredit those who are le-

gitimate. *Nor will it do so.* The honest psychic or medium
has nothing to fear from this book. It can only help him by
making it harder for the fakes, cheats, and liars to continue their nefarious work and confuse the sincere seeker.
The only medium threatened by this book is the fraudulent one.

My basic attitude toward mediumship and psychic phenomena in general is that historically taken by the Church.
Long ago, wary of the dangers of psychic dabbling, the
Church openly discouraged the mourner from seeking
communication with deceased loved ones and instead
stressed the reality of *communion* with the dead. This is the
"communion of saints." We the living are linked to the so-
called dead in God's fellowship of love. Attempts to go
beyond communion to overt communication, however, as
through a medium, can become a dangerous addiction.

But in trying to avoid extremes for the good of souls, the
Church went too far and unfortunately abandoned some
of its own mystical heritage. It so downgraded the reality
of personal psychic experiences—which have happened
spontaneously to millions of believing Christians—that un-
wittingly it played into the hands of those who would
exploit man's natural hunger for mystery for their own
purposes. My firm opinion is that much of the current ex-
cessive fascination with mystery, especially by young
people, results from the Church's aloofness toward the
true, profound, and wonderful mysteries which lie at the
heart of spiritual experience.

This is why I have taken a strong lead in urging the
Church to rediscover its mystical and psychical roots—not
to strengthen belief in the psychic, as such, but to strength-
en belief in the Church's message that there is a spiritual
world, that man is part of it, and that Time is the ante-
chamber of Eternity.

However, I have spent almost as much energy in trying

to combat the abuses of psychic experience as in trying to win the Church back to an acceptance of the validity of such experience. It is precisely because I believe so deeply in the psychic dimension that I detest those who pervert and misuse it to their own advantage: namely, phony mediums. These desecrators of the holy, these blasphemers of the dead, are psychic parasites battening on the sorrow of the bereaved.

This remarkable, unique book is the testament of one such fraudulent medium who lived for thirteen years in darkness and then emerged into the light. It is a spiritual story, not in the goody-goody sense, but in the most profound meaning of that word, because it tells how a man came to feel that he had gained the whole world but lost his soul.

When I first met M. Lamar Keene, through my Masonic brother, William A. Twiss, he had been in virtual seclusion for three years. That time had been spent, as this book tells, trying to disentangle himself emotionally from the sticky web of lies, deceit, and fraud in which he was trapped for so long.

As Lamar unfolded his experiences to me, I sensed how vital it was that this book be written. When I invited Allen Spraggett to collaborate as a professional writer and a psychic investigator, he agreed that Lamar Keene's story was too important not to be told.

Those who read this book will have, I trust, ears to hear and eyes to see, and will not be like the believers in Madame Flora's phony wonders who, even after being told they were phony, clamored:

> Please let us have our séance,
>   Madame Flora!
> Just let us hear it once more,
>   Madame Flora!

This is the only joy we have in our lives,
   Madame Flora!
Our little dead are waiting for us,
   Madame Flora!
You wouldn't keep us away from them
   would you, Madame Flora?
Please let us have our séance,
   Madame Flora!
Let us just have it once more,
   just once more, Madame Flora!

I commend this book to the truth-seeking reader, confident that "ye shall know the truth and the truth shall make you free."

PREFACE

Allen Spraggett

In William Lindsay Gresham's novel *Nightmare Alley* (often seen on the Late, Late Show in its movie version, starring Tyrone Power), the antihero is a cunning opportunist who climbs from carnival mind-reader to nightclub mentalist and then to minister of a fashionable and successful spiritualist church.

As a successful spook merchant, Gresham's memorable character Stan Carlisle, enjoys money, adulation, and the attentions of desirable women. He becomes suave, sophisticated, and smooth as silk, but inside is the heart of the carny who used to laugh at the geek—the poor wino in every sideshow, at the bottom of the heap, who impersonates the Wild Man of Borneo and bites the heads off chickens.

Stan Carlisle cheats, lies, wheedles, and seduces his way to the top. Then he meets someone—a steely woman psychiatrist, in this case—who outcheats, outlies, outwheedles, and outseduces him and sends him plunging all the way down the ladder again.

Gresham's bitter and biting story ends with the former

medium, once at home in the salons of the rich and famous, back at the carnival begging for a job. And what's offered him? To be a geek, of course. . . .

This book, with some important differences, is *Nightmare Alley* in real life. It's about a nonfictional Stan Carlisle who enjoyed unusual success from his phony medium's bag of tricks. But in this true-life version, the protagonist sickens of the whole mess, turns from it, and makes a new beginning.

As a writer I find his story a marvelously gutsy, colorful, and compelling account. As a psychic investigator I think it's one that's important to everybody with a serious interest in parapsychology and the unexplained.

Read the true story of Lamar Keene and the nightmare alley he inhabited as a fake medium. It's a story I'm sure you won't soon forget. . . .

1/MIRACLES DELUXE

In this day of rampant psychic wonders, what's the most mind-boggling you've heard about?

Uri Geller, perhaps, bending spoons with his eyes? Or the famed Philippine psychic surgeons who remove everything from ingrown toenails to gallstones with their bare hands?

Or is the most amazing thing the uncanny power of spirit mediums like Arthur Ford who can pick out of an audience a perfect stranger and astound him with facts from his own genealogy (including the great-aunt nobody liked to talk about who was crazy for cats and had a sex-change operation at age seventy)?

Well, such phenomena are pretty impressive. However, compared to the feats I performed routinely as one of the world's highest-paid mediums, they shrink to exceedingly modest proportions.

Clairvoyance? I was better than Kreskin.

Mind over matter? In my presence objects not only bent, they defied gravity.

9

Psychic healing? My spirit guides majored in it.

My mediumship represented the ultimate in seance room razzle-dazzle. In my séances, a mysterious substance called ectoplasm purportedly emanated from my body. Ectoplasm has been variously described by true believers as having the consistency of chewing gum, of appearing as a shimmering white haze, or of feeling as solid as metal.

My particular ectoplasm, which apparently streamed from various orifices of my body in cascading billows, was dazzling white and, on the occasions when sitters were allowed to touch it, was reported as having the feel of fabric in some cases and of flesh in others.

Ectoplasm is vital to physical mediumship ("physical" meaning the movement and influencing of objects in contrast to "mental" mediumship involving such feats as mind-reading) because it is this mysterious substance in which the spirits of the dead clothe themselves to appear in tangible, bodily form. Such ectoplasmic spirit figures are called materializations. I specialized in spectacular materializations!

I also majored in trumpet mediumship. This involves the use of a tin trumpet, to amplify the spirit voices, through which the departed communicate audibly with the living. Sometimes the sitters say that the spirit voice is identical to what it was when the person was alive in the flesh.

During a trumpet séance the tin megaphone is levitated—that is, it floats through the air under its own power. This can be very impressive and I was the most impressive trumpet levitator around.

I also majored in producing "apports"—gifts from the spirits which sometimes materialized out of thin air and at other times tumbled out of the floating trumpet into the sitter's lap.

In the area of mental mediumship I was just as adept. In my séances total strangers received spirit messages so evidential, so crammed with personal details, that the sitter's skepticism collapsed like a punctured balloon.

Mere boasting on my part? You're forgiven for thinking so (I admit to having a hefty ego), but then judge for yourself. Consider some typical incidents from my medium's casebook.

On March 13, 1966, Rose Johnson was attending the Sunday evening service of the church where I was then co-pastor, the New Age Assembly in Tampa, Florida. She heard me say from the pulpit, "People are always misplacing things. Who here has lost something?"

Most of the 250 people in the church raised their hands, including Rose Johnson, who had lost her library card a couple of weeks before and, being an avid reader (mainly of psychic books), keenly missed it. As a matter of fact, she had already asked her spirit guides to help her find it.

"Mrs. Johnson," I said, pointing to her, "would you come forward?"

"I was overwhelmed," she wrote later in a formal statement (which I have before me) "and wondered what on earth or in heaven was going to happen to me.

"Mr. Keene asked me in front of the congregation what I had lost and I told him my library card.

"He requested that the congregation sing a hymn of faith to help raise the power. I stood watching Mr. Keene, who had his eyes half-shut in a semitrance.

"Suddenly, as quick as that, something fell at my feet. It just seemed to come right out of thin air. I picked it up. It was my lost library card!"

A loud "Oh!" rose from the congregation, followed by applause. The hand was for me and for the spirits who through my mediumship had rescued that lost library card from wherever it was and returned it to its owner—in the twinkling of an eye.

Rose Johnson was impressed enough to substantially increase her givings to the church.

Another recipient of a psychic miracle, a retired businessman named Robert Black, was impressed by this kind of phenomena to the extent of writing a check to the church for a thousand dollars! That particular supernatural wonder, according to the signed and witnessed statement I have before me, took place in April, 1966.

Bob Black had attended my séances a few times and was very interested, though still skeptical. The spirits decided to demolish his doubts.

During a Sunday evening service I singled him out, asking him to stand. The regulars in the congregation inched forward on their chairs, sensing that another psychic bombshell was about to explode.

At my request, Black stood in the church aisle, where two women members faced him, clutching in their outstretched hands an open Bible provided by someone in the congregation. As I waited quietly for the spirits to move, my eyes closed, and the two women said they could feel tremendous "vibrations" in the Bible. This, I explained, was the psychic energy building up.

Suddenly something seemed to leap out of the pages of the Bible. It fell to the floor. Bob Black picked it up and blanched.

"This . . . this is my . . . my Masonic advisory council membership card," he stammered. "But how? . . . where?

"I always carry this with me. In my wallet. It *never* leaves my wallet."

"Well, check," I said quietly.

He opened his billfold—and the card was gone.

The congregation applauded this fresh display of the

spirits' fantastic power, through my mediumship, of "dematerializing" an object in one place and, a split second later, "rematerializing" it elsewhere. But sweeter than the applause was the sound of Bob Black writing his thousand-dollar check.

Such phenomena became so common in my séances that I seemed to be running a sort of astral Lost and Found department.

One woman, in a statement dated September, 1965, and signed by five witnesses, declared that through my mediumship the spirits returned "the same flowered cloisonné pillbox I lost six months ago." A man named Tom Behmke attested on May 8, 1966, that the gold watch-chain which "precipitated" into his hands during a séance in full light was "the one worn by my father who is now in spirit" and had been missing for years. Thirty-five witnesses signed his statement that the chain "dropped into my outstretched hands seeming to come from thin air."

Spirit messages? Mine were so uncanny that they made the hair rise on the back of people's necks.

Here is a letter, written in longhand by a Chicago woman, a sincere spiritualist, who visited my church for the first time during a Florida vacation in April, 1969.

"Words cannot express our amazement and joy at your wonderful, wonderful demonstrations of spirit power," she wrote.

"During that Palm Sunday service, though my husband and I had never before been in your church, you gave us spirit messages not only for ourselves but for several of our friends back here in Chicago. Some of the things you said about our friends were unknown to us, and you said to check them out and let you know.

"Well, Sarah Deacon was speechless when she listened to the tape-recording of the service and heard you mention her by name, as well as her parents, loved ones in spirit, her spirit guides—even her social security number!

"She immediately started looking for her social security card to check the number you gave. She said, 'How could the spirits find it a thousand miles away when I can't even find it in my own wallet!'

"Well, Sarah did find it, and you gave the nine-digit number absolutely correctly.

"You must be about the most amazing medium in the world today!"

I must confess that, reading that letter, I was inclined to agree with the writer. . . .

My congregations, which were always full houses, didn't dare skip a single service or séance for fear of missing something new. As a medium, I was Mr. Versatility. Every psychic wonder I unveiled was more dazzling than the last.

"The spirits like to keep us guessing," I used to tell my congregation, "because they have a sense of humor."

One night I was demonstrating billet-reading, in which, blindfolded, I "read" and answered written questions from the audience, when a masculine voice at the back of the church said in a loud whisper, "The guy's a bloody wizard."

"Well, if that's so," I responded, picking up the cue, "let's see what I can do."

As though under a sudden spirit inspiration, I took a glass of water from the pulpit, poured the contents over some flowers, and then, wrapping the empty glass in a handkerchief, smashed it against the side of the pulpit. There was the sound of glass shattering.

The congregation gasped. They gasped louder, however, when I opened the handkerchief to show the jagged shards of glass, then calmly took one, popped it into my mouth, crunched on it, and swallowed it.

A sort of groan went through the congregation. One

woman fainted. Later, several people confessed that they thought my zeal had carried me too far, that I was tempting the spirits, and they had been on the verge of rushing forward to prevent my killing myself.

"We were in a state of shock," said one man. "But what happened then made us feel ashamed of our own lack of faith."

What happened was that I didn't fall to the floor clutching my stomach and blood spurting from my mouth, as many of them had feared, but continued the service with no visible discomfort from having eaten the mouthful of glass. Later, incredulous church members crowded around to examine the leftover jagged pieces on the pulpit and went away shaking their heads.

"Spirit protection," I assured them, "is a wonderful reality to those of us who are called to the sacred work of mediumship."

Were these mind-blowing feats produced by the agency of departed spirits, as my followers devoutly believed?

Or were they the result of mysterious psychic powers generated in my own unconscious mind?

Neither.

Every one of the multiply witnessed wonders I've described, and many more, were fraudulent. Hoaxes. Tricks.

Mind you, not exactly the sort of tricks you'll find in your corner magic shop—but tricks nonetheless.

How, exactly, did I accomplish them?

Well, that's a good question, and one I myself sometimes ponder with considerable amazement.

How *did* I, for example, outwit the self-styled psychic investigator who tried to catch me literally red-handed by coating my trumpet with a telltale dye that would stick to my fingers?

And how, in the name of Houdini's ghost, did I confound other *mediums*, fellow practitioners in the black art of extrasensory deception? Many of them begged me to sell them my secrets, including my favorite, the talking trumpet which the sitter could actually hold on his lap and feel, as well as hear, the vibration of the spirit voices issuing from it.

The how, what and, most important, the *why* of my career as a phony medium is what this book is all about. The inner workings of all my wonders are unveiled in these pages.

In addition, and more significant, are the revelations—sure to sound unbelievable to some—about a network of organized mediumistic espionage in the United States: a psychic mafia that takes in millions of dollars a year.

What is the psychology of phony mediums? How do they see themselves and others, especially their sitters or clients?

Are mediumistic frauds genuinely religious in their own screwed-up way? Or atheistic? Nihilistic? Do they believe anything—or nothing?

Since they can hardly run an ad under Help Wanted, how are new mediums recruited? What's the process of psychological seduction which produces a full-fledged practitioner of the art of impersonating the dead?

What about the money? How good is it? Can a medium become a millionaire from bringing back the dead?

What about sex in the séance room? Are there, as rumored, mediums who specialize in a special form of "grief therapy" (an in-depth form) from which they reap commensurate rewards, monetary and otherwise?

Are there any *genuine* mediums? Have I ever experienced a real psychic or spirit manifestation?

Finally, and possibly most interesting of all, why do phony mediums flourish bigger and better than ever despite previous exposés? What is it that drives victims of mediumistic chicanery back into that dark room where they suspect, or sometimes even know for a certainty, that they've been defrauded in the past?

For the answers to these questions, read on. And fasten your seat belt; it's going to be a wild ride. . . .

2/THE MAKING OF A MEDIUM: How it all started

Mediums, if you were wondering, do not combust out of a cloud of ectoplasm; they come into the world by the same route as everybody else.

And they are *made* mediums, not born that way (though, to be sure, mediumship can run in families and, as this book reveals, may even start in childhood).

I wasn't born with a silver trumpet in my mouth. My parents, ordinary middle-class people in Tampa (my mother died when I was thirteen), had no interest in spooks or spiritualism, and I don't think I even knew what a medium was until my late teens.

I was raised a Baptist to the age of sixteen and then became a member of the Church of Christ. From my early years I'd felt a strong religious impulse and for a while considered entering the ministry.

However, I ended up going to business college, and working full-time besides to pay for my studies.

My first job was in a grocery store, then behind a soda fountain, then in the restaurant business, where I quickly rose to managerial level and by the time I was nineteen was making $250 a week. Not bad for a teenager.

It was then that came my introduction to spiritualism—one that changed my life more dramatically and profoundly than I could possibly have imagined.

I met a boyhood friend—Raoul, we'll call him—who had gone away to a Pentecostal Bible school in South Carolina to become an evangelist. But Raoul told me how he had given up the sawdust trail and now had a deep interest in spiritualism.

His interest was sparked, he said, by an elderly gentleman he had met when he was at school (Holmes Bible College in Greenville, South Carolina). The old guy had been a short-change artist for a circus and had attended séances by the score. He knew many mediums, believed in psychic forces, and was a member of the Rosicrucians. In his Bible classes Raoul was being taught that spiritualism was of the Devil, but his elderly friend urged him to look into it for himself.

"Maybe you'll change your thinking," he said.

Prophetic words.

Raoul had attended a few séances, was intrigued and wanted to see more, and invited me to join him. And that's how it all started. . . .

We attended public services at Tampa's biggest spiritualist church where a married couple, Mildred and Martin Baxter, were the co-pastors and resident mediums.

Looking back, those first encounters with the unseen were quite impressive. Mildred Baxter, a tall, imposing-looking woman with a refined voice (she had trained to be an opera singer but didn't make it), stood on the platform and gave members of the congregation "messages from the other side." The accuracy of these often elicited gasps of astonishment and admiration from the recipient. In time Raoul and I received a few spirit messages, and they too, though not particularly spectacular, were accurate enough to be impressive.

Besides the regular Sunday services, we attended séances held periodically by the Baxters. In these the manifestations ran the whole range of so-called "physical" phenomena. Virtually always in the dark, spirit faces were "precipitated" on silk; spirit writing appeared on previously blank cards; diaphanous, undulating spirit-forms "materialized" from ectoplasm, a mysterious psychic substance drawn from the medium's body; and the voices of the dead spoke from a tin trumpet which seemed to float around the room under its own power.

The Baxters were skillful mediums, the séances impressively done, and in the beginning both Raoul and I believed. I was the first to have suspicions about the genuineness of the physical phenomena while still believing that the "mental" phenomena—the clairvoyant messages from spirits—were real. I probably felt then that the mediums were acting basically in good faith and simply wanted to strengthen belief in what they knew to be true: namely, the philosophy of spiritualism.

It was the first trumpet sitting that convinced me the physical demonstrations were fakes—pious fakes, if you like, but fakes.

When I expressed my conclusion to Raoul, he disagreed. He was still an all-the-way believer, though shaky. I was a part-way believer, in an odd state of mind comparable perhaps to that of the fundamentally sincere evangelist who publicly overestimates the attendance figures at his rallies for the glory of God.

Raoul and I joined private classes the Baxters held for those who wanted to develop their own latent psychic powers (so latent, in most cases, as to be undetectable). These

classes were very popular (doesn't everyone want to be
psychic and eventually to be his own medium?) and, for
the Baxters, very lucrative.

Mildred dwelt a great deal in her instruction on the importance of reading as widely as possible if we were to become successful mediums. This, she said, would enable the
spirit entities to speak intelligently to sitters who came for
advice—the principle being that they, the spirits, would
draw from our minds.

"It's like a fine instrument," she said, "being desirable in
the production of a great musical composition. That is to
say, one would not expect a great composition to be played
upon a broken-down, out-of-tune piano."

Some of the subjects she suggested boning up on were
basic law, diet and nutrition, comparative religion, and
medicine. When I became a medium I understood the importance of these, because they are the most common
areas in which people ask the spirit guides for advice.

(One of the most alarming things about the mediumistic
racket is how completely some people put their lives into
the hands of ill-educated, emotionally unbalanced individuals who claim a hot line to heaven. As a medium I
was routinely asked about business decisions, marital problems, whether to have an abortion, how to improve sexual
performance, and similar intimate and important subjects.
That people who ask such questions of a medium are risk-
ing their mental, moral, and monetary health is a shocking
but quite accurate description of the matter.)

By the time we had sat in the Baxters' development class
for a year (without developing very much except an almost
infinite capacity for enduring boredom), Raoul and I were
ready to launch out on our own.

Were we then sincere spiritualists?

Yes—halfway at least. In the spook business, as we were

soon to discover, mediums are divided into two classes: the "shut-eyes" and the "opens."

The shut-eyes were the simple believers, often sweet little old ladies (although not all old ladies in spiritualism are sweet) who genuinely felt that they were psychic and able to pick up "vibrations." They were kept around by the others because their transparent sincerity was good for public relations. But the shut-eyes were not let in on the tricks of the trade.

The open mediums, by contrast, were those who knew they were frauds and admitted it—at least in the secret circles of the fraternity.

When Raoul and I started out, we would have had to be classed somewhere in between the shut-eyes and the open mediums. We were in fact what is called in the business "open to ourselves." This meant we knew that some mediums were total frauds—though we didn't know how many—but the fraud, we felt, was for a good cause and didn't do anybody any harm. If it strengthened faith, could it be that bad?

We also believed that some mediums did get genuine vibrations from the unseen world and that that was what really counted. Even if some of *these* mediums sometimes gave the spirits a helping hand by doing prior research, the important thing ultimately was that the true and noble philosophy of spiritualism be advanced.

We really thought, in the beginning, that we *could* pick up messages psychically. We decided to set ourselves up as mediums who would teach the exalted truths of spiritualism—the Golden Rule, salvation through character, and eternal progression—and stick to clairvoyant messages. We didn't intend to stoop to producing physical phenomena. If people want trumpets and ectoplasm, we said, nobly but naïvely, let them go elsewhere.

We soon discovered that the shut-eye medium, even if his eyes are half-open, doesn't stand much chance compared to the physical medium in attracting customers. People *want* spirit forms, spirit voices, spirit photographs, and similar wonders—and isn't the customer always right?

As I think back now, trying to recapture the mood and the experiences of those early days in the ghost business, I realize afresh how murky the psychology of mediumship is.

Take Raoul and me. We started out, as I've said, basically sincere, but our thinking belonged to that dark gray area in which we were willing to remember names and bits of information picked up in conversation and later weave them into spirit messages while at the same time believing that we also got impressions from the psychic ether. We were sincere fakes. Or maybe schizophrenic would be more accurate.

Perhaps our mental state wasn't all that different from the attitude of the State Department official who lies in the interests of national security or steals classified information and passes it to the press because he disagrees with government policy. Or from that of the copywriter for a big ad agency who shades the truth in his client's favor. Or. . . . well, there are many other respectable people who, so to speak, do wrong for the right reasons.

None of this is to try to extenuate what I did as a fake medium. Of that I remain deeply ashamed. But perhaps we should see it in perspective as being different in degree, but not necessarily in kind, from much laundered larceny in our society.

At any rate, from a psychological viewpoint I think that Raoul and I were healthier when we renounced our halfway position and became out-and-out frauds, and that wasn't long in coming.

We took over a spiritualist church in a small town not far from Tampa. Soon we wanted to branch out. We knew that others in the mediumistic business were earning big money, but to do the same we needed contacts. The stars of the psychic vaudeville circuit were associated with the booming spiritualist camps, chiefly Chesterfield in Chesterfield, Indiana and Silver Belle in Ephrata, Pennsylvania, where every summer thousands of pilgrims plunked down cash on the line to talk to their beloved dead. (Later we discovered that the annual take at Chesterfield was at least a million dollars, and that long before inflation!)

Our mediumistic mentor, Mildred Baxter, had a fit when we suggested to her contacting either Chesterfield or Silver Belle. Later we found out why. Years earlier when she was just starting out as a medium, she had gotten into a row with Ethel Post Parrish, the queen bee of Silver Belle, been declared forever *persona non grata* there, and tossed out on her ear. Twenty-five years had done nothing to cool Ethel's rage.

Raoul and I decided to dump the Baxters—they had been useful to us, but we were ready for better things— and hitch our ectoplasm to a new star. We determined to get a foot firmly in the door at the camps.

We went to see a noted medium, Viola Osgood Dunne, who was a rival of the Baxters and a pillar of Camp Chesterfield. A hearty, obese woman, neither bright nor stupid (like most mediums), she welcomed us, when she heard we were students of the Baxters, with open arms. Few things give a medium more joy than stealing another's protégés.

In our first meetings with Viola and two of her mediumistic co-workers, the question of fraud wasn't brought out into the open. There was some polite sparring. They tried to feel us out, to discover just how much we knew, and we did the same. Neither of us learned much. We still didn't know whether Viola and her satellites were shut-eyes (which seemed unlikely), open to themselves (that is, only half-fake), or wide-open.

I was betting that Viola Osgood Dunne was as wide open as you could get. Raoul, however, thought she might be basically sincere. We decided to find out by watching one of her psychic demonstrations. We invited her to "serve" (a spiritualist term) our church. If she used tricks, I was confident I'd spot them.

Well, she came, she demonstrated—and she cheated like hell. There was a large turnout because Viola Osgood Dunne was one of the big names of the spiritualist world. And she gave a very professional demonstration of billet-reading: that is to say, answering written questions submitted in sealed envelopes by members of the audience.

Reading questions inside a sealed envelope takes a little doing, of course, but Viola's psychic powers were more than up to it. She used the "one ahead method," as it's called, which is considerably older than the hills but, as she showed, still effective when done by a pro.

Her technique was simply to get hold of one of the questions, in any one of several possible ways, and to use that for the first question. In other words, holding the sealed envelope against her forehead, as though tuning into the etheric vibrations, she recited the question she had previously filched as though it were the one inside the envelope. When the question was acknowledged by the person who had written it, she gave some standard spiritualistic answer ("The spirits tell me yes and no and say you will understand it in due time"), then tore open the envelope, scanned the question inside, as though satisfying herself that it was the one she had just answered, and then went on to use *it* as her next question.

The good medium, of course, is resourceful and adaptable, and Viola fleshed out her performance by drawing on

her previous knowledge of six or seven veteran spiritualists in the audience. Altogether she did a good job.

When it was over I asked Raoul; "Well, what do you say
now?"

"You were right," he replied.

That was in 1958. It marked our transition from the twi-
light of half-fraud into the darkness of total fraud.

The next time we saw Viola, which we made sure was
soon, I simply said to her, "You did a very good job for us,
but of course we should have supplied you with advance
information. However, we weren't sure exactly how you
worked."

That broke the ice. She invited Raoul and me to do clairvoyance in her thriving church and opened her files to us
for prior research. The files were a gold mine. Viola Osgood Dunne had traveled all over the United States and in
several other countries calling up the dead, and she had
files on thousands of sitters who had attended her séances.
These files she made available to members of the psychic
mafia in other cities. It is this swapping of information on
sitters—many of them séance freaks for whom dark rooms
have an irresistible attraction wherever they happen to
be—which enabled me in Florida to tell veteran spiritualists from Chicago, say, or Los Angeles startlingly accurate
things about themselves and their departed loved ones.

The web of mediumistic espionage that spans the United States and to some extent other countries is what makes
the spook racket more than merely a local phenomenon
and truly a Freemasonry of evil: a psychic *mafia*.

Viola Osgood Dunne's files were mainly on index cards
kept in locked metal filing cabinets. (Much later, after we'd
gotten to know her better, Viola appointed us protectors
of her files in the event of her sudden and unexpected
demise. In a letter she wrote to me December 29, 1966, she
said; "I am leaving to fly north and in case something

unexpected should happen to me I have asked Eliza [her housekeeper] to contact you, so you could take care of certain personal matters for me.

"In the chest in my room are some files; a few boxes and a black, long letter file are in the second drawer of the gray chest in my bathroom; and in the cabinet section of the steel desk in my Florida room are some books, etc. . . . "

The discreet wording was in case the letter was read by someone for whom it wasn't intended. The files were some of her mediumistic records which would have been incriminating if found by friends or members of her family who were not in on the deception. Yes, *members of her family*. It's not all that unusual, we found, for mediums to keep their fraudulent practices a secret even from their own spouses!

Another letter before me was written by Jennette Rykert Sadwin of Miami, in her own hand, on August. 30, 1967. It contains tips on some of her followers who were planning to come to Tampa for sittings with us—tips which enabled me to wow them at their first seance—and also has some revealing allusions to her new husband, Phil, who obviously wasn't in on her deep, dark secrets.

"As Phil is out with some friends playing cards," she wrote, "it is a good time to get this letter off to you. . . . "

"I have to be careful before Phil. But you know we always find a way, eh!"

Later, she concludes; "Must hurry and mail this before Phil gets home. . . . "

Among themselves, mediums often refer to their files on sitters as their "poems" or "poetry."

Unlike many admirers of the great medium Arthur Ford, I wasn't shocked to read in his biography (*Arthur Ford : The Man Who Talked with the Dead*, by Allen Spraggett with William V. Rauscher) that according to his secretary he kept "poems" which he read before a séance. You see, among the files Viola Dunne gave me were a number of notebooks on sitters in various cities which she said originally had belonged to Ford.

The code used by mediums in their files is simple. Some of the common conventions are: A cross beside a name means the individual is dead; a circle, that he's alive. A heart next to a name indicates someone with who the sitter is or once was in love. "G.G." next to "Blue Star" would mean that a medium had assigned the sitter a girl spirit-guide named Blue Star.

I'm looking at this moment at an index card with "poems" on it, sent to me by a medium in another city in advance of some of her followers coming to me for a first-time sitting. I'll reproduce some of the "poetry" as it appears:

"Coral Long Hofer. . . . Mother O Minnie Averitt. . . . Father O Horace Averitt. . . .

"Blind in one eye . . . had operation in the bad eye but it was not to restore sight. . . .

"Grndmther x Mary Jane Scott. . . . Grndfther O been running around. . . . This disturbs Carol's mother. . . . The grndmther died from a disease that she couldn't get well from. . . . Grndfther's name is Clifton. . . .

"Fr. of Father Herman Whipple X. . . . Fr.'s mother was named Wilharber. . . ."

This medium's notes were not as organized and concise as I would have liked, but at the time she was just a beginner. Anyway, give a good medium the few bits and pieces of personalia you just read, and he could build it into a monumental case for spirit survival. Think how evidential it would be for an unsuspecting sitter to be told by a medium she had never even seen before that her father was blind in one eye and had had an operation on it, though not to restore the sight.

How amazingly detailed! How explicit and accurate!

"There's no way the medium could have know that," the sitter would tell her friends in absolute sincerity.

The secret of the medium's marvellous "hits" were spies, not spirits!

Raoul and I were stretching our mediumistic wings, and our church was too small to hold us. So we simply gave it up and walked away, leaving church and people without a pastor.

Our aim was still to get a piece of the action at Camp Chesterfield, where the financial pickings were best. But becoming a Chesterfield medium wasn't easy. The establishment there ran a closed shop, and no wonder—the take, as we eventually discovered, was even better than we had imagined. We couldn't simply gatecrash Chesterfield, bulldoze our way in, because even if we had gotten past some of the dimwits on the board we'd never have handled the incredible woman who ran it all—Mable Riffle.

She was the most colorful, fantastic character I met in the zany world of spooksville. Only five feet tall but as tough as steel, with the vocabulary of a longshoreman and the guts of a sword-swallower, she was one formidable customer!

One of my most typical memories of Mable Riffle when we later got to know her was of her, then in her seventies, scooting around Camp Chesterfield on a golf cart and stopping periodically to have a shouting match with her leg. One of her legs used to swell and pain and she wouldn't be able to hop on and off her scooter as fast as she liked. So she would pound that bad leg with both fists, cursing it, commanding it to walk smartly and do what she told it to do, as though the leg were another person and not part of herself at all. She treated other people the way she treated that leg: obey or else!

There are many great stories about Mable. One told

how she and her husband Arthur, with another medium, Edith Stillwell, were driving to serve a spiritualist church somewhere. Arthur lost control of the car, a brand new Chrysler, and it plowed off the road and was totally wrecked.

As always, Mable appeared first, clambering out of the wreckage and inquiring vigorously as to whether Arthur and Edith were all right. Yes, both were fine. But Arthur was bemoaning the accident.

"Mable," he wailed, "the car's a complete loss."

"Oh shit, Art," she said, "that's all right. We'll get a new one!"

And she hustled them out onto the road to start flagging down a ride so they could get to that spiritualist church that was waiting for them.

I think the only thing Mable would have been afraid of was a real ghost. She herself told me how one night she and Arthur arrived home late. While he was parking the car, Mable started up the steps of the front porch. Suddenly she gave a bloodcurdling scream.

Arthur came running and found her white-faced.

"My God," she said, "just as I was going up the steps, I saw this form standing there in the shadows. It was like a spirit or ghost."

"Well, what's wrong," said her husband with nice irony, "you bring them back in your séance room all day and night, so why be frightened?"

"Yeah," said Mable, "but I just don't want the damned things jumping out at me!"

But we were not to get to know Mable for a little while, and in the meantime Raoul and I opened a church in Tampa.

It's very easy to set up a church and obtain the legal right to call yourself "Reverend." A lawyer was needed who, for three hundred dollars, drew up the articles of incorporation. We had eight charter members (true-blue believers who had attended our séances and been overwhelmed), and that was enough to form a board of directors.

We started holding services in the Federated Woman's Club Building in Tampa, which had a seating capacity of about seventy five. Almost at once we were filled to overflowing, and by the end of the first year we were purchasing property and beginning to build our own edifice.

We called it the Good Shepherd Universal Spiritualist Church. It was all tax-free, of course, and in the articles of incorporation, approved by the Florida secretary of state, we could give ourselves virtually any power, authority, or title we wanted. I, who had never taken a theological course, proceeded to conduct weddings and funerals, ordain others to the spiritualist clergy (for a price), run a religious school, and certify other congregations that might wish to affiliate with us. I never gave myself a degree, though many other mediums did and styled themselves "the Reverend Doctor." In the eyes of the law I had as much ecclesiastical status as the Archbishop of Canterbury or the Pope—and it was all a racket!

Our church services had a touch of revivalism about them. We emphasized healing, and my partner, Raoul, with his evangelistic background, liked to imitate Oral Roberts, who was then casting out devils and making the lame walk every Sunday on television.

I remember one woman who was a chronic complainer. She had every disease she had read about in her medical encyclopedia. Though she looked fit and strong to me, she always hobbled in on a cane.

Her husband brought her to one of our healing services, and Raoul decided to do an Oral Roberts on her. He pulled out all the stops. He prayed a dynamic prayer throbbing with emotionalism, then slapped his hand on her brow and shouted, "Be healed! Now put down your cane and walk!"

"I don't know whether I can," the woman quavered.

Raoul grabbed the cane out of her hand and broke it in half across his knee. Now she had no choice but to walk without it. And walk she did—down the aisle and right out of the church. We never saw her again, but the fun was worth it.

And the money. . . .

Well, it poured in. I discovered that people will pay any price to communicate with their dead loved ones.

I remember a woman who came to our first service, Bertha Jenkins, who had lost her only son. She was thrilled beyond measure to find that through my mediumship she could talk to her beloved Jack. Until then her life had been hopeless. We put the stars back in her sky—and she repaid us amply.

Though she wore tennis shoes and dressed like a ragpicker, she gave large amounts to the church—which is to say, to Raoul and me. If she was pleased with a sitting, she would leave two hundred dollars. And when we started talking about building a church edifice, she called me to her home and handed me a paper bag. It contained six thousand dollars. (She believed there was only five thousand dollars, but we kept the extra and didn't tell her.)

In eight months Bertha gave us another five thousand dollars and, of course, her son in spirit, Jack, always encouraged her in the good work she was doing. Before Jack was through with his mother, she had given us thousands of dollars.

Eventually she became a little suspicious of Jack's repeated urgings that she give even more to the church. Possibly I was overeager and had pushed too hard. At one point during a séance she said, "Jack, I want you to call me what you used to call me."

I knew it was a test. The only thing I could do then was to laugh and put her off by having Jack say, "I'm going to surprise you one of these days and do that."

When Bertha left I thought, How the hell am I supposed to find out what it is she wants to hear? She was too good a touch to lose, so I was determined to give her what she wanted. But what was it?

Both Raoul and I dug desperately. We tried to find out her ethnic background, the origin of her name, but that didn't yield any clues. Meanwhile Bertha's givings, we noticed, had dropped off.

Finally, one night a group of us from the church went to her house for a social evening. During the proceedings I became conveniently ill, a headache you know, and Bertha insisted I take an aspirin and lie down in her bedroom to rest. As soon as she left me alone, I was out of bed. Somewhere in that house, I knew, probably in that very room, there had to be the information I needed.

Well, I found it. In Bertha's family Bible, which was in the dresser drawer next to the bed. Her middle name, Lona, it turned out, was a nickname for Apalonia. That, I felt sure, was the clue I needed.

I researched Apalonia and found it to be the name of a saint who was famous for curing toothaches. My hunch told me that this was it! I decided to gamble.

At the next séance her departed son, Jack, recited the names of all the other members of her family—which I'd copied from the family Bible—and then called her Apalonia, saying he was getting "the vibrations of a toothache."

That did it! She was completely satisfied and, her faith in my mediumship reconfirmed, the generous donations resumed. And her case was typical of many.

With practice, of course, my mediumistic skills improved. I made a habit of carrying a small notepad in my pocket and jotting down every casual remark which would help provide evidential messages. Rarely did I use such information soon after picking it up. The rule was to wait—until the individual had forgotten everything about the conversation and then out of the blue, spring on him some juicy evidential morsel which he himself had provided.

Early in my mediumship I decided to excel over other emissaries of the unseen by the detailed and explicit nature of my clairvoyance. I went in for social security numbers, insurance policy serial numbers, and even numbers of unlisted bank accounts!

How did I get such information?

Simple. I became an expert pickpocket.

It was even easier than that, most of the time, when all that was required was for Raoul or me—depending on which of us was conducting the séance—to lift a woman's purse—in the total darkness while she was occupied listening to spirit voices from the trumpet—take it into another room, and go through it. Later the purse was returned to the same spot, and when the séance concluded and the lights came on, the woman suspected nothing.

This method yielded not only social security card numbers and other confidential data, but also many of the personal objects which the spirits later returned as "apports." The sitter probably didn't miss the tiny religious emblem we removed from her purse for—what?—a few days, a week? By that time she couldn't possibly connect its disappearance to the séance, but would assume that she had lost it somewhere while pulling other objects out of her purse. We let a few weeks or months elapse, and then one night during a séance the spirits would announce, "We have a gift for you," and the missing religious emblem tumbled into the woman's hands.

The miracle was even more spectacular if, as often happened, the sitter *asked* the spirits for help in finding her missing cross or necklace or jeweled pill box or whatever.

Sometimes, if we were prepared, we returned it on the spot. That really wowed them: Ask the spirits about a lost article, they said, and it materializes a moment later! In other cases the spirits would promise, "We'll see what we can do," and at the very next séance the missing object was delivered by astral express.

Sometimes, in a variation that was particularly impressive, the spirits told the sitter exactly where she had *lost* the missing article. When the sitter hurried to the spot—in a busy downtown drugstore, perhaps, where we knew she often shopped—she found the object right where we had planted it a short time before. Sometimes people wouldn't even miss the object we pilfered, and when it was apported back to them they assumed that the spirits had dematerialized it out ot their purse or wallet or wherever and rematerialized it before their eyes. That was how I did the trick with the businessman (mentioned in the first chapter) who swore that his lodge card, which *"never* leaves my wallet," had been miraculously transported from it into the pages of the open Bible before him.

Recently, while watching television, I heard a psychic who's very popular with show business people relate how a well-known pop singer called him for help in finding a lost ring. The medium said he had told her the ring was frozen in an ice cube in her refrigerator— and guess what? It was.

This reminded me of a couple of minor miracles we pulled. We hired a guy to deliver flowers to a family we were setting up for a demonstration of spirit power with instructions that he lift some small object and bring it to us. He pocketed an expensive religious medallion. Later the spirits returned the medallion to the owner, who expressed very generous thanks.

Even better, and closer to the incident the television psychic described, was one in which we instructed our stooge to pick up some small object while he was delivering flowers and hide it somewhere in the house where the occupants would be very unlikely to find it. He took a diamond dinner ring and slipped it into a crevice behind the stone mantel in the living room.

It wasn't long before the ring's owner, a devoted follower of ours, called me almost in tears because she had lost something that meant a great deal to her. Could the spirits possibly find it?

Over the phone I tuned in to the etheric vibrations and told her that what I was getting sounded strange but nevertheless she might take a peek *behind* the top of the mantel.

She returned to the phone ecstatic, filled with praises for her wonderful spirit people and for me, their humble servant.

The apports in full light which numerous witnesses said came "out of thin air" were produced by misdirecting the onlookers' attention—raising one hand dramatically or, simpler still, having them reverently bow their heads —while I skillfully dropped or tossed the object with my other hand.

It sounds incredibly easy, I know—*too* easy—but I was never caught. Believe me and all the magicians who've told you so: the hand *is* quicker than the eye!

Strange as it may sound, we had a Catholic nun once at a group séance, and she received an apport which was a small statue of the Virgin Mary. She was thrilled, took it to a priest, and he began attending our séances. He received evidence which, he gave us to believe, convinced him of the truth of spirit communication.

Clergy of other churches attended our séances, too, though often, like Nicodemus visiting Jesus, they came by night. Many of them became believers in the great truth of spirit return.

Eventually our success grew until we were able to open a

glittering new church of our own in Tampa. And at about the same time the gates of Camp Chesterfield swung open for us. With a little encouragement from our side.

That ushered in a whole new episode in my adventures in the spook business. . . .

3/HIGH CAMP AMONG THE SPIRITS, or Who Grabbed My Ectoplasm?

In July, 1960, the spiritualist world was rocked by an explosion that sent shock waves through every séance room in the country and shivers up every medium's spine.

It has become known as the Great Camp Chesterfield Exposé.

What happened was so crazy, so zany, that apart from a Peter Sellers movie it could only happen in the weird and wacky world of the psychic.

Two sympathetic researchers, Tom O'Neill and Dr. Andrija Puharich, had tried to get the first motion pictures ever of the materialization of a spirit. O'Neill was a believing spiritualist, editor of the monthly newspaper *Psychic Observer,* an ordained minister of the Indiana Association of Spiritualists (the legal entity which owns and runs Chesterfield), and a close friend of Marble Riffle and other stalwarts at the camp. Puharich was a physician and psychical researcher whom O'Neill had recruited to give the project scientific credibility.

With the enthusiastic support of the Camp Chesterfield

39

authorities, O'Neill and Puharich went into a dark séance room equipped with infrared lights and film (and a snooperscope, a device developed by the United States Army for making night vision possible on the battlefield) and shot the materialization of a ghost. The medium was Edith Stillwell—one of the true greats of Chesterfield, famed for her multiple-figure materializations—and her cabinet attendant (or bodyguard) was none other than the high priestess of Chesterfield, Mable Riffle herself.

The researchers were not underhanded in the least (after all, they believed in psychic phenomena, especially O'Neill, and both Edith Stillwell and Mable Riffle were told exactly what the infrared film would do—make any figures in the totally dark room stand out as clearly as in the light of day—and were allowed to take a peek for themselves through the snooperscope. This should have alerted them, but unaccountably they went ahead with the project).

The experiment was a disaster for the spiritualists. Peering through the snooperscope in the dark, Puharich saw that what were supposed to be spirit forms of shimmering ectoplasm materializing out of thin air, were actually figures wrapped in chiffon entering the séance room through a hidden door from an adjacent apartment.

The infrared motion picture confirmed Puharich's observations. There, etched unmistakably on the film, were the familiar faces of camp mediums, dressed up in gauze, impersonating departed spirits.

Tom O'Neill, the devout spiritualist, was devastated by the revelations. He who had believed implicitly in the phenomena now raged against "the frauds, fakes and fantasies of the Chesterfield Spiritualist camp!"

The July 10, 1960, issue of the *Psychic Observer* bore the headline: WE ARE IN MOURNING, THE TRAGIC DECEPTIONS IN MATERIALIZATION.

"Writing this just about tears my heart out of its socket,"

O'Neill declared in the lead article, "but the story must be written and our film must be publicized!"

The magazine reproduced stills from the infrared film which showed spirit forms, and next to them photographs of Homer Watkins and Peninah Umbach, both Camp Chesterfield staff mediums.

"These mediums look enough like the spirits to be their twins," said the *Psychic Observer.*

Writing in the following issue of the newspaper, Andrija Puharich called Chesterfield "a psychic circus without equal!"

The resultant controversy was traumatic for some in the spiritualist movement. Tom O'Neill, who resigned from the spiritualist ministry over the incident, died not too long after—partly, so many believed, from a broken heart. His paper, *Psychic Observer,* declined drastically when the spiritualist churches which had provided most of its subscribers and advertising revenue, instead of rallying around O'Neill as he had hoped and expected, boycotted him.

Why condemn O'Neill rather than the Chesterfield fakery?

Well, some spiritualists said that they didn't believe the exposé, that O'Neill had sold out to the Catholics or other enemies of spiritualism and had framed the mediums. Others said that even if the accusations were true, O'Neill should have kept quiet for the good of the movement.

In the furor over the O'Neill incident, I saw our chance to establish a foothold in the Promised Land. We ostentatiously rushed to the defense of Camp Chesterfield.

We used all kinds of explanations to conjure away the damning film footage that showed the spirits using a secret door. It was all "trick photography," we told our people, and of course the spirit communicators backed us up in our séances. That was good enough for our followers!

It worked. What we had undevoutly hoped for came to pass when Mable Riffle, considering us heroes for having defended her beloved Camp Chesterfield in its hour of need (though the exposé, rather than ruining business, actually improved it), invited us to join the staff as accredited mediums. At last!

My first day at Chesterfield I was walking on the green, well-treed grounds thinking of the money to be made when a commanding voice shouted, *"Lamar, c'mere!"*

It was Mable Riffle, Chesterfield personified. She roared up on her electric golf cart with a fringe-covered top and whisked me off on a whirlwind tour of the Coney Island of spiritualism.

She showed me the substantial buildings, some of them (like the main auditorium, called the Cathedral) quite impressive; the many acres of grounds; the medium's homes, mostly on one street ("Medium's row," it's called); the cafeteria; the three hotels; and, all the while, talked nonstop about every phase of the camp's operation. She told me the files were kept beneath the Cathedral and took me there to show them to me.

They were voluminous. There were billetsized cards and papers, from every service or public séance ever held at Chesterfield. The files were arranged alphabetically by geographic location—cities, states, countries. Each contained the name of the person and the question asked. There must have been tens of thousands of individual index cards.

The files also included personal objects, keepsakes, clipped to individual cards. These were "apports" to be returned to the sitter the next time he visited the camp. Think how impressed that farmer from Pumpkin Creek, Michigan, would be when during his second visit to Chesterfield he received from the spirits the very tie-clip he had not seen for he couldn't remember how long!

Most of the buildings at Chesterfield, I discovered, had been donated by believing spiritualists, often single donors. The cafeteria and the cathedral were built by money given by a Howard Maxon. There is a Dr. Hett Memorial Museum, an impressive stone building housing psychic artifacts and memorabilia (such as twenty-five oil paintings by the famed mediums the Bang Sisters). It also was a gift.

Chesterfield is spiritualism's answer to Disneyland. That first season of mine, more than 65,000 pilgrims crowded onto the grounds from here, there, and everywhere. They spent more than a million dollars to commune with their beloved dead.

And they had a wide selection of modes of communication from which to choose; trumpet seances, materializations, clairvoyance, spirit card writing, apports, spirit photographs, and spirit precipitations on silk.

The fees varied. For a group sitting, which often ran from twenty-five to as many as a hundred sitters, I charged a minimum of three dollars per person and as high as ten dollars. For materializations the going rate was twenty five dollars, but the sitter often gave more, especially if the manifestations were above average (as mine always were).

At the height of the season I was giving as many as twenty-five sittings daily and taking in as much as a thousand dollars per day. It gave me a great thrill!

Eventually I became so popular at Chesterfield that the voting faithful—which state law required must include all members, including laymen, of the Indiana Association of Spiritualists—unanimously elected me to the camp's board of trustees. This, I might add, was over the jealous opposition of most of my fellow mediums (who in this case failed to manipulate the lay membership as easily as they usually did).

I was also made a trustee of the Universal Spiritualist Association, one of the largest clergy-ordaining and church-chartering organizations (about two hundred affiliated congregations at that time) in American Spiritualism. *I was, make no mistake, no mere mediumistic freelancer but a key figure in the mainstream of spiritualism in the United States.*

The long-term contacts made at Chesterfield could be even more valuable that the immediate rewards. A woman I met there ultimately gave my partner and me more than sixty thousand dollars.

People were frantic for contacts with the other side. One woman would have booked a sitting with me every day if I had allowed it (I didn't—it was too much work coming up with new information on her). She spent the entire summer at the camp.

Some people, I found, were so desperate for the assurance of continued relationships with the dead that they sought and found sex in the séance room. This is a murky subject which I'll wade into in a later chapter, but let me say here that some spiritualists do become so obsessed that, as one medium put it, "they'll even lay a goddamn ghost!"

I stayed away from the more exotic forms of mediumship, such as sex séances, but otherwise was extremely versatile in the phenomena I produced. My trumpet sittings were better than anybody else's, and the other mediums at Chesterfield cordially hated me for it.

I used a trumpet with luminous bands on it so that in the darkness, relieved by only a single red bulb, the sitters could see the trumpet apparently floating around the room while numerous distinctly different spirit voices issued from it.

The voices, of course, were all me. I was a helluva good ventriloquist! But how did the trumpet float?

Simplicity itself. In Chapter Five I describe in detail the secrets of the séance room, so it's sufficient to indicate here that the tin trumpets that mediums use come in sections and are extendable to about four feet. That gives enough length to swing the trumpet through a wide arc, producing a variety of impressive gyrations and loop-the-loops. Meanwhile, the voices as a rule are coming from a different trumpet altogether; a second, smaller one which the medium has in his other hand, and which, because it has no luminous bands around it, is invisible to the sitters in the near-total darkness.

My materializations were tremendously popular because, again, I gave them something extra. In my séances, lit by a red bulb (we needed total or near-total darkness, we said, because white light was harmful to the ectoplasm), several forms of various shapes and sizes appeared simultaneously. They undulated, shimmered, vanished, reappeared, and usually made their final exit by melting through the floor or dissolving like a puff of smoke.

Sounds impressive, and it was—in the dark—but the secrets, as you'll discover in Chapter Five, are ludicrously simple.

My billet-reading was spectacular, too. Again I went beyond the typical medium, adding a color, a style, a showmanship.

Before receiving the written questions from the audience, I would have my eyes taped and then bound with a heavy black blindfold. Under these conditions I'd proceed effortlessly to read the questions and give the answers from the spirits.

The secret here was the old mentalist standby: the peek down the side of the nose. No matter how securely the eyes are blindfolded, it's always possible to get enough of a gap to read material held close to the body. Yet what I was doing *looked* impossible.

What kind of people went to Camp Chesterfield?
Most of them, in my book, had dubious claim to the ad-

jective *normal* but some were weirder than others. The strangest and most pathetic were the astral necrophiles mentioned earlier who craved sexual contact with their departed spouse, lover, or whatnot. But there were other weirdos, too.

One sitter of mine insisted on talking to a spirit she called Daisy. I let her talk (when in doubt, let the sitter tip you off) and discovered that Daisy was her departed French poodle.

Another sitter absolutely insisted on getting a spectacular message, so I told her that in 1980 she was going to make a trip to Bimini and there find a secret temple in which she would recover some sacred jewels! That seemed to satisfy her.

One medium's husband dealt in dubious antiques. With his wife's help he sold a credulous woman, with more money than brains, an ordinary communion chalice as the authentic Holy Grail! Price two thousand dollars.

There was one little old lady at Chesterfield who, because of education or dentures, used to say "I just love to come to this *spiritless* camp!"

We mediums all laughed about it, remarking, "If she only knew."

Of course, if the sitters are weird, the mediums are weirder. In the madhouse of spiritualism, mediumship is the ward for incurables.

It's hard for me to convey to the reader the strange, schizoid state of mind of some of the mediums at Camp Chesterfield. A few seemed actually to be trying to pretend to themselves that they weren't frauds!

Once, during a backroom discussion, when I used the word fraud, a woman medium whose materializations were as phony as a three-dollar bill whirled and said, "Don't use that word when I'm around. I certainly believe in what I'm doing!"

So I sidled up to her, stared her in the eyes, and said,

"Okay baby. Let me take away all your chiffon and gauze and then go into the séance room and do your stuff! And I want to be there!"

She sniffed, and stalked off.

Most mediums are women and they are strange customers. As a rule they're highly-sexed and domineering. It takes drive and stamina to succeed in the ghost racket and the typical female medium comes on like a ten-ton truck!

Most seem to marry more than once, and they always carry the name of the previous husband. So you get a whole procession of noted mediums with three names: Rosemary Jackson Thomas, Marie Doyle Perkins, Mary Murphy Lydy, Nina Challen Richards, and Mary Langley Beatty.

Of the woman mediums I knew, most had the physical constitution of a horse. They could go all day and night doing sittings, readings, seances, services—as long as the pay was right.

Mediums live under great tension. They are estranged personalities because of the nature of their work—cheating people. Loneliness and secrecy are a way of life for them. They can't afford to have close friendships, except with other mediums, and these are rarely if ever true friendships. The spirit of professional competition is too great.

As a matter of fact, the rivalry and jealousy among mediums is almost unbelievable. Each one wants to be better than the other and, of course, to make more money. And I was no different.

The only reason mediums band together is for mutual protection.

"Let's face it," Viola Osgood Dunne said after the great Chesterfield exposé, "if we don't hang together we'll all hang separately."

Mediums protected each other (because by so doing

they were protecting themselves), especially when it came to troublemakers. Every season at Chesterfield there was a certain quota of "grabbers":—would-be debunkers who reach out in the dark and grab the materialized spirit form. We mediums banded together against this species of pest.

If a medium was grabbed in a séance, she (usually it was a woman) would warn the others, "Watch out for so-and-so. That goddamned sonofabitch grabbed me!" This news traveled like wildfire through the camp.

A notice would be placed in the Chesterfield file room or on the mediums' bulletin board. A known grabber wouldn't be allowed into a séance. If he was particularly persistent or obnoxious, he'd be escorted off the campground—maybe with a kick to help him on his way.

Mable Riffle had her own way of dealing with skeptics, whether they were grabbers or nongrabbers. Once a couple on the grounds of Chesterfield was loudly talking about fraud at the camp and Mable overhead them. She simply went up to the couple, all five feet of her, and snarled, "Let me tell you something. We do not have that kind of talk here. Now you get your goddamn ass off these hallowed grounds and don't ever come back!"

They went.

There was a woman newspaper reporter, remembered only as Rosie, who wrote a scathing series of articles on Camp Chesterfield depicting it as a sort of psychic freak show. Mable of course was enraged, as were all the mediums, and the word went out that under no circumstances was Rosie to be allowed on the camp grounds again.

However, Rosie was nothing if not resourceful. The next year, intending no doubt to do a sequel, she decked herself out in a fright wig and turned up at a séance presided over by none other than Mable Riffle herself.

No sooner had the spirit voices started coming from the

trumpet than Rosie started demeaning them. Mable recognized her voice immediately. On went the lights and Mable went for Rosie.

Grabbing the reporter by the back of the neck, she ushered her up a steep flight of stairs, kicking her in the rump on each step and cursing her with every profanity imaginable. Rosie was hurled into the night with the warning never to show her face at Chesterfield again. But Rosie was a tough customer, almost as tough as Mable. One summer she showed up at Chesterfield, in another of her disguises, and Mable spotted her. Rushing over, Mable grabbed Rosie's arm in a viselike grip and, cursing her furiously, started dragging her bodily to the camp gate.

Just as they reached the gate, some very good financial supporters of Chesterfield arrived. In a flash, Mable changed her tone.

"Goodbye, Rosie dear," she said, smiling sweetly, "we'll be seeing you again some time."

But that was the last we ever saw of Rosie.

The fact that some mediums conceal their fraudulence even from their spouses was mentioned in Chapter Two. On one occasion a medium at Chesterfield went to Mable Riffle and expressed fears that her husband was going to catch on sooner or later, possibly sooner. Mable's reaction was typical. She called the husband to her office.

"Floyd," she said, "this is the way we do it around here," and proceeded to tell him everything—the files, the chiffon ectoplasm, the apports bought by the crate, and so on.

She concluded, "Now if you go out of here and say anything about this to anybody—well, you're just a goddamned liar!"

The man, who was six foot three—Mable was barely five foot—went away without a word. And his wife continued her mediumship.

How does a medium react if she's grabbed or exposed?

Well, there's a right way and a wrong way. The wrong way was exemplified by a medium at Chesterfield named Etta Scott Bletsoe who, giving a trumpet sitting in total darkness, simply sat on a table in the center of the room and spoke through the trumpet. She had her eyes shut so that when a sitter suddenly turned on the lights she, being oblivious of the fact, continued to sit there droning on through the trumpet. Then she opened her eyes, realized what had happened, and blurted out, "Oh my God, we've been caught!"

(The same medium showed greater presence of mind on another occasion when, while giving a clairvoyant demonstration at Chesterfield, she saw from a window an outdoor privy going up in flames and exclaimed, "Jesus Christ!" Recovering immediately, she smiled sweetly and said, "Pardon me, friends, but I felt His presence so near I just had to speak His name.")

The right way to react to exposure was demonstrated by the most unflappable medium of them all, Mighty Mable. Once she was in the dark talking through a trumpet and the lights suddenly came on. She too had her eyes shut tight and went right on talking.

When she opened he eyes the sitter (there was only one) was looking at her.

"Mable," the sitter said, "you were talking through the trumpet."

Without batting an eyelash, the old pro deadpanned, "I was being controlled by a spirit and he was using my body and vocal cords rather than building a voice box from ectoplasm."

So there!

The rule was: when you think you're caught admit nothing and brazen it through.

Fanchion Harwood Dorsch was a well-known Chesterfield materialization medium who impressed a lot of people (including noted author Marcus Bach in his book *The Will to Believe*). Fanchion developed a line all her own to explain away in advance any possible exposure.

"There are several kinds of materialization," she told the sitters before every seance. "There are materialization, etherealization, transfiguration, and impersonation. These are all genuine phases of mediumship."

If somebody grabbed her ectoplasm and found not a spirit but the medium, Fanchion blamed it on impersonation. A spirit tricked her, masqueraded as her (or whatever—the details were more than a little vague). Anyway, it got her off the hook, at least in her own eyes and those of the true believers.

A near-escape we had once in a house sitting taught Raoul and me never to lose our nerve in the face of apparent exposure. If nothing else, the bad eyes of the faithful may save you.

In this particular séance in a private home, I had moved, in pitch darkness, to the piano to provide some spirit background music while Raoul spoke through the trumpet. A split second after I returned to my place, someone going to the bathroom flipped on a light. I was safely seated, though just in the nick of time, but Raoul was caught standing, the trumpet held to his lips.

In an instant I grabbed him and pulled him down next to me, and as I did, he dropped the trumpet.

The hostess (as it turned out, the only one who was looking) didn't see that. What she saw, she said, was the most amazing sight her eyes had ever beheld.

"There was the trumpet suspended in mid-air," she told the others, "and when the light came on it just fell to the floor."

How did *we* deal with grabbers?

Well, Raoul and I never had to contend with one, though we did have our share of sitters who were more outspokenly suspicious than most. My tactics with them were brutally direct.

I remember a woman who owned a chain of health spas and came to one of my Camp Chesterfield materializations with a friend. Maybe I wasn't up to my usual form that day. At any rate, this woman said to me as she left: "I would have thought you could have gotten much better material. You're not even a good fraud."

Waiting for a moment until the others were out of hearing, I hissed, "There's the goddamn door and it swings two ways and you use it to get the hell out of here and don't ever come back!"

She blanched, her lips quivered, and she turned and stalked off.

Then I turned back to the other sitters with a warm, gracious smile to accept their congratulations on a magnificent séance.

As my mediumship developed more maturity (or became riper and rottener if you like), I developed adeptness in anticipating and heading off the question of fraud and in converting suspicious sitters.

Once, entering the séance room for a trumpet sitting, I caught a glimpse of something peeking out of a woman's purse. Realizing it was the microphone of a tape-recorder (we banned the use of recorders except with the spirits' express permission), I caught myself before mentioning it. I had thought of a neat way to turn the situation to my advantage.

Later, in the pitch darkness of the séance, the spirit voices suddenly said, "We know you have an unauthorized tape-recorder. We see it clearly!"

The woman was flabbergasted, and any incipient skepticism was turned into firmer belief.

We constantly looked for ways of maximizing credibility

and strengthening the faithful in their faith. One way was to have our spirit guides disagree with us.

Raoul's guide or special spirit teacher (we likened them to the "guardian angels" in the Bible) was Dr. Robinson, a cultured English physician defunct on the mundane plane for a century or so. Mine was an irreverent girl spirit named Clementine (most mediums have at least one child guide—perhaps because they, the mediums, are childish). We and our guides disagreed on several issues, the favorite being reincarnation.

The guides were teaching the doctrine for a long time while we pretended to be undecided about its merits, sometimes openly questioning it during séances in a friendly argument with the spirits. Finally, after milking this routine for as long as we could, we capitulated and accepted reincarnation.

People thought these guide-medium conflicts were very evidential because they reflected two really different personalities. This fascinated them.

Another very effective way of defusing skepticism was to use "plants": people hired to attend a service or a séance posing as blatant debunkers.

Sometimes we would have the intruder object verbally to the proceedings and denounce us as fakes. Sometimes, more subtly, we would have him write a billet and then appear to be reluctant to put it in the basket to be passed up to the medium. We would have him place the billet in his pocket and then of course we, without even touching it, proceeded to read and answer his question clairvoyantly!

Sometimes we were understanding of the stranger's skepticism and forgave him, sending him away humble and contrite. Other times we blasted him for his sacrilege and ordered him out of the church never to return.

Winos were especially good as stooges. They worked cheap and if, later, they had ever decided to inform on us, who would have believed them?

We had ready excuses, plausible or implausible (depending on your viewpoint) for any number of problems that might arise on our mediumship. For example, if somebody who was still alive inadvertently turned up in a séance, our standard alibi was that he was probably asleep at that time and had left his body, "taken an astral trip," without realizing it.

There were risks in many of the methods we used, but with our experience in handling people and the wall of fanatical credulity that our followers had built around us (I think they would have lynched anybody who seriously tried to disrupt a service or séance), we felt supremely confident.

Other mediums were not so confident, however. Fanchion Harwood Dorsch, the materializing medium, would never give sitters apports, cards, pictures on silk, or spirit photographs, and she opposed other mediums doing so. Her objection was that nothing should be handed out in a séance that could possibly be used in court as tangible evidence against us.

A medium named Paula Philips had all her files typed, on the advice of her attorney, to avoid possible prosecution for conspiracy to defraud if they were confiscated. The attorney's view was that the files were less incriminating typed than in the medium's own handwriting.

Every medium, no matter how clever, is accused at one time or another of being a fraud. But the good medium learns how to react, how to handle people, including nuisances.

Once Marie Doyle Perkins, a real mediumistic veteran, had a group for a séance who turned out to be Bible school students, hardcore fundamentalists who were convinced that she and all mediums were in league with the Devil. What was the point of going on with the sitting? The money wasn't that good. So Marie looked for a logical out—and found it.

One of the students picked up her trumpet and started talking through it. With that the medium put on her most diabetic smile and said, "Please, I can't possibly give you a séance now. Why, that's sacrilege. Don't you realize that the trumpet is as sacred and meaningful to me as the Communion cup is to you!"

My way out of a séance that wasn't going right was simply to have the spirits decide the vibrations were bad and call the whole thing off. The spirits took the responsibility, not me.

By the way, fundamentalist opposition to spiritualism is good for business. When we were in our first church, the Seventh Day Adventists ran huge ads in the local paper warning people against spiritualism and so-called churches where ghosts appeared and trumpets talked. To them, of course, it was all perfectly real, but diabolical rather than divine. As a result of the ads, our business boomed! (You might say that, on the subject of the psychic, the spiritualists are crazy and the fundamentalists are stupid).

There were some mediums so bizarre that they weren't welcome even at Chesterfield. One was named Nina Ward Hughes. She claimed that Jesus Christ was her personal spirit guide. When the dinner table was set in her house, there was always a third place for Christ. Mable Riffle said, "Nina's nuts!"

As for Mable herself—well, she was sensible and shrewd, as mediums go. In style she was unpretentious. Her spirit guide, for example, was an ordinary guy with an ordinary name—Henry Williams. And on that a funny story hangs.

Mable told me, incredulously, how once in Indianapolis

while walking to a car park, she saw a little black boy and had a strong impulse to speak to him.

"Hi sonny," she said, "how are you?"

"Fine," the youngster replied.

Mable then asked, "What's your name?"

The boy stared up at her and said, "Henry Williams." The same name as Mabel's guide.

"Can you beat that?" she laughed, slapping her thigh as she told me about it.

These crazy coincidences can be seized by the smart medium and turned to his profit—in one case, forty thousand dollars profit.

At the time, Raoul and I were thinking of buying property in the country for a church ranch, so we called a realtor and went with him to look at some acreage that was for sale. What we saw had great possibilities. The realtor said, "I'm selling this for the Minnie Barrett estate."

A tingle went through me. As it happened, Minnie Barrett had been a member of our church, and her family still were members, but we hadn't known that she owned extensive property.

At the next séance at which her family was present, the spirit of Minnie spoke and told the heirs to give the forty acres to the church. And we got it!

The approach we took was that Minnie's spirit had impressed us to contact that particular realtor in the first place, and he confirmed that indeed we had called him first. By this combination of coincidence and shrewdness, not only was the property ours, but the family had to pay the realtor's 10 percent commission!

Most of the Chesterfield mediums were zany but some were zanier than others.

One medium named Ralph Whitney developed a fast-paced, racy style of giving messages that ususally kept the audience howling. He told a woman that he saw around her an electrical storm within the past month. She said yes, that was true.

Then he said, "Well, I see a bolt of lightning that went right between your legs and burnt all the feathers off your canary bird!"

The congregation broke up, including the woman. It turned out that lightning did strike and kill her canary, but nobody's spirits could have said it just the way Ralph's did.

He was also an exceedingly accomplished ventriloquist who used to get messages from spirit voices that spoke intermittently out of the air. The range of these voices in timbre and diction was startling, and they seemed to come from just above his head, from the left, then from the right, then from behind him. Audiences found this "direct voice" phenomenon very striking.

Other mediums were less striking—even to the intellectually underprivileged types who frequented Camp Chesterfield. One exceptionally dumb medium was giving a séance in which Master Teachers—exalted beings from the seventh astral plane—materialized and lectured. The medium brought through an Egyptian master.

"But Master teacher," said one of the sitters, "you have a Southern accent."

The spirit replied, "I'm from the southern part of Egypt."

There's no way of accurately computing the money from which people were separated at Chesterfield.

One of the saddest stories was of a woman who gave a large sum to the camp because of spirit urgings through Mable Riffle. Then she returned home and found that her house had burned to the ground. She came back to the camp and asked Mable if she could redeem part of the donation. Mable flatly refused.

What do mediums really believe?

On the basis of my experience I'd say that most of them believe nothing. Their lives are empty of faith in anything except the buck.

At Chesterfield nothing was sacred. People were things to be used. The Bible is exhibited in most spiritualist churches but in their hearts mediums scorn it—and openly too, when they're with their own kind.

The jokes about Jesus' virgin birth were many and varied but had one thing in common: their scabrous quality.

A group of us were talking one night after the suckers had gone and we could let our ectoplasm down. One woman medium said, "Now that bitch Mary was smart, making Joseph do without while she screwed around. And even when she got knocked up she lied her way out of it. No wonder Jesus wound up as an open medium!"

My partner, Raoul, used to quip, "Poor Jesus, he didn't get paid for walking on the water."

One of the Scriptures Raoul and I liked best for parodying was I Samuel 28, the story of King Saul seeking to call up the ghost of Samuel through the Witch of Endor. We said we were going to write a spiritualist opera based on that story, and we often ad-libbed some of the dialogue as we traveled together, driving in the car, say. Sometimes I'd be Saul and Raoul would be the Witch, or vice versa. Sample dialogue:

THE WITCH: Hark, hark, whom shall I bring up to thee?

SAUL: You stupid bitch, you're like all the other mediums! You don't even know who I want to talk to!

THE WITCH: First cross my palm with silver!

SAUL: Bring me up Samuel!

THE WITCH: I'm beginning to put two and two together—

you're the King! You've deceived me before I could deceive you. . . .

It wasn't going to be much of an opera, but the scenario was pure spiritualism: crude and crass.

All mediums, including me, subscribed to the creed that a new sucker is born every thirty seconds and that the typical spiritualist believer is in sympathy with his own destruction. For our sitters—even those with whom we pretended friendship outside the séance room—we had unspeakable contempt.

One long-time medium at Chesterfied who specialized in spirit images impregnated on silk— a simpler-than-simple technique that I'll explain in the chapter on the secrets of the séance—was so contemptuous of the sitters' intelligence that he opposed my attempts to upgrade the evidential quality of the phenomena. As he saw it, the sitters didn't deserve even convincing fraud. The cheapest, silliest, most palpable fakery was more than good enough for them. At one mediums' get-together (or shouting match) he inveighed against my giving people social security numbers, credit card information, and other explicitly evidential messages.

"You give them too damn much," he roared. "You can never please these crazy bastards. Eventually the only way you'll be able to draw a crowd is to stand on the roof of the Cathedral, drink gasoline, and recite the Gettysburg Address with a flaming torch sticking up your ass!"

All mediums would agree with what Clifford Bias once said at Chesterfield (in private, of course): "Wars, depressions, personal and national disasters spell prosperity for us." The present economic stresses in the United States are good news for the medium.

What about mediums and the chief commodity they deal in—death? What was their real attitude toward the subject about which they talked, preached, and exhorted day after day?

Well, when medium Mary Hunter's husband died and his remains were on view in the casket in the Camp Chesterfield Cathedral, she ran to the front and pulled at the corpse, begging him to come out. That shows the depth of faith of one who had been marketing it to others.

Mable Riffle's husband was trimming a tree in front of the Cathedral one day when a branch broke and he fell, breaking his neck. He died on the spot.

They called Mable. She came running, saw what had happened, and turned on the tree. She raged at it, cursed it, kicked it, and beat it with her fists, shouting obscenities.

Then she ordered workmen to come and destroy it. She stayed until they had cut and blasted that tree out of the ground.

This was the spiritualist leader displaying her faith in life after death.

A quasi-official document put out by Chesterfield, "The Medium's Handbook," oozes the sort of sanctimonious bilge that nauseated me. Written by a nitwit of a man who ran the camp for a while after Mable Riffle's death, this document represents the epitome of pious hypocrisy.

Article Three in "The Medium's Handbook" says, "Camp Chesterfield prays, hopes and intends to give the very best presentation of Spiritualism and psychic phenomena to its members, friends and visitors. Camp Chesterfield wants only the best—in its speakers, teachers, mental and physical mediums, healers, workers and helpers. You are expected to strive for and live up to this appellation—'the best.'"

Article Four is worse: "Love God above all. God is Infinite Intelligence and expresses in that which is Good, that which is True, and that which is Beautiful. This must come before family, relatives, friends, money, prestige, health, comfort, convenience; in fact, before and above all else."

Worse still, Article Five: "I am a Spiritualist. First, last and always, I am a Spiritualist. I am proud and not ashamed to be a Spiritualist, yet I am humble and deeply grateful to God for this wonderful truth. Strive to live up to your highest concept of our religion—preach it, practise it, live it, *be* it—practise what you preach and preach what you practise."

"The Medium's Handbook" is never quite as unctuous and absurd as when it lectures the Chesterfield staff on proper diction and decorum.

"Continue your education. Never stop learning. The ideal Spiritualist minister-medium is a well-balanced, well-informed person with a wide range of interests, not an ignorant, narrow-minded, bigoted, prejudiced, supercilious, and egotistical provincial.

"GOOD ENGLISH. Not one of us is perfect. We all make errors, including grammaticatical ones. But please, please, please, learn and use the rudiments of grammar. 'WE Spiritualists are proud of our religion,' not 'US Spiritualists are, etc.' 'God give US Spiritualists,' not 'to WE Spiritualists.' 'It is I who am knocking,' not 'It is me.' 'You and I are going,' not 'you and me.' The plural of 'you' is 'you' *not* 'you-uns.' ' "

(This instruction in simple grammar was wasted on the Chesterfield mediums, most of whom couldn't parse a sentence. Looking over the letters I have from Mable Riffle and Ethel Post Parrish, a pair of the biggest names in spiritualism, I note that both ladies were totally innocent of the rules of syntax. There is hardly a comma, period, or capital in either letter; they are each one interminable sentence!)

In some items in "The Medium's Handbook" we can detect the old mediumistic rivalry raising its head. The medium who wrote the immortal document loathed and detest-

ed another medium, a woman, who had the habit of pro-
nouncing *spiritualism* with an overlong, rolling *r*. The Medium's Handbook" tees off on this.

"Spiritualism," it intones, "is a five-syllable word, there-
fore is neither pronounced SPURT-yul-ism nor SPIRT-
tulism. It is quite proper to say 'Spidditualism.' *provided* the
rest of your language follows the English-Scottish pronun-
ciation of the letter 'r', as 'diddigible' for 'dirigible.' 'inhed-
dit' for 'inherit' and 'teddible' for 'terrible.' Affectations of
speech are easily discernible and usually cause amusement
or irritation rather than admiration."

To one who knew what a psychic sideshow Camp Chesterfield was, the following admonitions were enough to in-
duce biliousness: "Camp Chesterfield is a Religious Institution, not a Street Carnival nor Amusement Park.
Please limit your signs to one name and one announce-
ment board of your activities. More than two signs will not
be tolerated. Neither is Camp Chesterfield a circus nor a
Night Club."

That last remark may have been a dig at me, since I was
sometimes accused by the other mediums of acting and
dressing more like a show business personality than a
psychic emissary. I wore colorful capes with high collars,
patent leather shoes with rhinestone buckles, and glistening
white suits. What the hell—I *was* in show business!

My wardrobe no doubt was the target of this shaft from
"The Medium's Handbook": "Camp Chesterfield expects
its ministers, mediums and workers to be well-dressed and
well-groomed. But please, no theatrical costumes."

There's an addition: "Men are to wear coat and tie at all
public services. No tennis shoes, please!"

As a quasi-official document, "The Medium's Handbook" no doubt would come into the possession of those
who were not mediums. Because its author anticipated
this, the language is always discreet and suitably cryptic in

spots. But knowing what you know now the reader can peer between the lines and discern the real meaning. Consider this gemlike passage:

"Please ask your guides to allot equal time to each sitter, not to permit many spirit visitors to one sitter and only a few to another. Apport mediums, *please ask your guides* to bring articles of equal worth to each sitter and not to bring only one of such articles as are usually in pairs (earrings or cufflinks, for instance).

"All mediums are *to warn their guides* NOT to suggest to sitters that only through that particular mediumship can 'highest' or 'true' spirit be contacted, can 'true development' take place, the particular mediumship is the 'best', or the medium should be given gifts or loans. Such will result in the cancellation of the medium's contract or lease!"

In other words, there's enough of the Chesterfield pie for everybody to have a piece; don't try to hog it all for yourself!

Could anything be more revoltingly revealing of the true nature of organized spiritualism today than this *official* document of America's leading spiritualist camp!

Lest you think that Chesterfield is now in eclipse or that its burlesques and excesses are, surely, too gross for any intelligent person to take seriously, consider Don Worley's article in *Fate* magazine (May, 1972). It's an account of his visit to Camp Chesterfield. Fully aware of the great O'Neill-Puharich exposé, Mr. Worley, who is obviously an intelligent man, nevertheless concluded after sitting with the Chesterfield mediums that many of them were "impressively accurate."

Of some of the mediums he met, Mr. Worley remarks, "I find it impossible to explain away [all that they did] in mundane terms. With these apparently sincere mediums I was not aware of any fraud and feel certain that the answer to their abilities does not lie in peeping through the tape and blindfold, nor in phenomenal memories of those members who return each year, nor in exchanging information, nor in any other such explanation."

He adds that his séances with physical mediums in dark rooms were "almost as impressive," and cites a convincing sitting with Virginia Leach Falls.

This woman, and the other mediums mentioned in the article, I knew at Chesterfield as part of the bunch—like me, full-fledged members of that fraternity of deception, the psychic mafia.

4/THE NAME OF THE GAME: MONEY, Or The spirits and Swiss Banks

As a medium, money never concerned me.

I mean that I didn't bother to think about it; there was no need. Money was simply there. More than enough for everything I desired.

We didn't concern ourselves with bookkeeping. If we wanted anything, we just took the money. We lived, as they say, high on the hog.

The good things of life abounded. Fancy clothes are a weakness of mine, and I had more suits than Liberace. I ate at the best restaurants and attended the best clubs. When I took out a girl, it was to the swankiest nightspots. It wasn't unusual to spend five hundred dollars for an evening on the town.

Within four years of starting in mediumship, my partner and I had paid $10,000 for two lots in Tampa and built a church ultimately worth some $100,000. For legal purposes the church trustees owned the building, but they were a rubber-stamp bunch. If anyone wasn't as pliable as putty, we quickly removed him.

Getting rid of "uncooperative" members was done with

absolutely no regard for human feelings. One elderly woman, Mary Belle Behmke, known to everybody in the church as "Aunt Mary," became the object of Raoul's anger after I—to anticipate the story—had renounced my mediumship and left the church. Mary, who had fetched and carried and worked tirelessly for the congregation for ten years, was excommunicated, was evicted from the small church-owned house she occupied, and ended up in an elderly folks' home in Michigan, where she soon died. Thus were treated those who dared to cross the master's will in spiritualism.

In any important decisions (important to us, that is), we as co-pastors had the spirit guides issue precise directions for the church trustees. Who would dare dispute spirit guidance? Certainly not our true believers.

By legal manipulation it wasn't hard for a medium to exercise even formal legal control of the church property if he or she so desired. In one case an older, established medium who owned her church outright sold it to us. We ran it for a while, then sold it out from under the congregation, leaving them with no church building and ourselves with a profit of twenty thousand dollars. All perfectly legal.

In addition to the church edifice, our group (meaning my partner and I) owned a New Age ranch outside Tampa that included a two-story lodge and several other buildings.

I personally owned a Spanish mansion on two waterfront lots in an exclusive section of Tampa, plus a house in St. Petersburg and an additional fifteen acres of land in southern California. My personal assets included more than $300,000 worth of property.

(When I left mediumship, I held an auction sale of antiques, art, and art objects largely acquired through my skills as a necromancer. We rented the livestock pavilion of the Florida State Fair Ground in Tampa and employed six auctioneers to sell around the clock, as long as people came. And they did—for five days and nights. Some auction! Some profit from mediumship!)

We didn't keep a complete set of books on our entire income. Only the spirits knew exactly how much we made, and there were times when even they weren't sure.

Mediums, even for professional predators, are an extremely avaricious lot. Two colleagues of mine, Eddy Mackey and Jimmy Lawson, told me they believed a medium should take something from *everyone* he met: "If you can't get anything else then take a book of matches!"

We took more than matches. And so did every medium I knew.

In our mediums' meetings at Camp Chesterfield and elsewhere, when we planned policy and strategy it was decided that none of us would run all our money through a bank account nor adopt any method that could be easily traced (or traced at all, if possible). The common thing was not to deposit in your bank account any more than you reported on your income tax. If one medium was caught with his hand in the till, we knew we'd all be suspected. Whatever we did with our money was our business, of course, but we were to think about the others as well as ourselves in avoiding detection.

Many mediums kept piles of cash. I knew one who had $25,000 for an emergency hidden in her attic. Many had safes. I know personally of two mediums who acquired numbered Swiss bank accounts. Ethel Post Parrish, the noted medium, was said to have a large private (very private) collection of diamonds—all real.

Most mediums tried to cultivate an impression, if not of poverty, then of a distinct lack of affluence. When Mable

Riffle died, though she had lots of dough, the family borrowed from Camp Chesterfield to finance the funeral. It was a way of covering up.

"Mable gave so much," said the eulogist, "and took so little."

The total annual take of organized spiritualism in the United States must be staggering. Think of the thriving camps, the hundreds of churches, the thousands of séances, sittings, readings, spirit healings, and other mediumistic consultations performed every year—for a fee. Think of my relatively small church in Tampa, about three hundred members, taking in ten or twenty thousand dollars in one night of services.

Also to be taken into account are the innumerable bequests to spiritualist organizations. For example, one Howard Maxon left several hundred thousand dollars to Camp Chesterfield, and another estate bequeathed it more than half a million. This money—nobody knows how much it amounts to—was and is administered by a board of trustees (mediums, that is).

When Mable Riffle was around she, and she alone, handled the money. Because of Chesterfield's financial muscle, she wielded considerable clout with the banks in neighboring cities, such as Anderson, where bank functionaries were only too willing to wait upon her. They recognized Mable—who was called "the goose that laid the golden egg"—as the mastermind behind a financial operation of more than modest proportions.

What does the average open medium make in a year? Nobody knows. Forty thousand dollars is a good bottom figure. No doubt incomes vary greatly, according to the skill and popularity of the medium, but the fact is that nobody on earth *knows* the truth about mediumistic incomes except the individuals themselves.

Much of my income came from gifts to me personally.

As I write, I'm looking at the statement of sale (dated December 28, 1966) of a piece of property which had been given to me by a pleased sitter. The property was worth $40,000 then, but I wanted quick cash, so I sold it for $16,500—pure profit.

One woman, who wasn't particularly well off, gave more than $40,000 to the church—to my partner and me—during the four years or so she attended. That wasn't unusual. I have numerous canceled checks made out to the church for sums of $1,000, $2,500, and $4,000. These often represented "love offerings" for a particularly comforting séance or series of séances.

Once people came to believe in our mediumship, they could be astonishingly generous. In playing upon their heartstrings I played upon their purse strings as well.

One evening I was doing blindfold billet-reading and gave a number of evidential messages to a middle-aged woman who was obviously deeply impressed.

On a hunch I said, "You received an impression just this evening while you were sitting there in your seat. Is that right?"

She replied, "Yes."

"Whatever that impression was," I said, "it's right; go ahead with it."

She answered, "Well, before I left home tonight I thought about writing a check for eight hundred dollars for the church and I was wondering if it was the right thing to do. Sitting here, as you gave me those wonderful messages, I had the strong impression to do it now."

An usher brought her check to the pulpit. And our bank account fattened a little bit more.

A technique for increasing the financial givings of followers was familiar to many mediums but used especially by one I knew. It was his custom to phone a sitter during the very early morning hours, rousing him or her from sleep. (At such a time the mind is particularly amenable to suggestion.) The medium identified himself as the sister's spirit guide and personal instructions followed, often pertaining, among other things, to increased financial generosity to the medium.

Thus was aided the student's spiritual progression and the medium's financial advancement, all in one phone call!

Seriously, this technique was responsible for lining more than one medium's pocket with dollars.

A favorite money-raising gimmick among mediums is "special projects." A phony worthwhile cause is established and people are urged to give specifically to it. Sometimes it's improvements to the church building (I've known a medium to collect money for a new roof and simply buy diamonds with it). Or how about the Christmas Cheer Fund for the Needy? The medium stands at the door after church services and receives cash. But none will find its way to the needy, believe me.

One Indiana medium had a very unusual sympathy project. He claimed to be working on an invention and to be guided by Thomas Edison. The invention was a sort of astral television set that would make possible mechanical communication wtih the spirit world.

This medium collected vast sums from the spiritualist faithful to complete the project. He even kept under lock and key a phony laboratory in case somebody got nosy and checked. You can be sure he'll be working on that invention for a long time!

Building projects are always good money-raisers. The idea is to start but never finish. One Sunday at our church I collected eighteen thousand dollars in contributions, most of them cash, for our building fund. At Camp Chesterfield there's a cornerstone near the Cathedral which says CHESTERFIELD COLLEGE, 19—. That's as far as it ever got.

That was where I picked up the idea for a sympathy project of ours: an orphanage and old people's home run by the New Age Assembly Church. My files contain old bankbooks representing a small fraction of the funds collected for this and similar fictitious charities. Many of the withdrawals went toward Thunderbirds, Cadillacs, cruises, my lavish wardrobe, entertainment, and my partner's exotic-animal collection.

At our church I collected one Sunday $18,000 in contributions, most of them cash, for our building fund.

One medium made some forty thousand dollars a year selling (technically, she asked for an offering) "blessed healing cloths"—cheap handkerchiefs over which she was supposed to have mumbled a prayer , magnetizing them with spirit power.

Occasionally a medium found an even crazier way to make money. Homer Watkins, a Chesterfield medium, told of a poor soul who sat in his psychic development classes week after week with an absolutely desperate desire to get the trumpet to float as the professionals did. He wanted that trumpet up in the air so badly he was almost beside himself.

The man, whom Homer described as "the dizziest, skinniest, palest, sickest guy you could imagine," had some money, so the medium said to him, "I'll guarantee you that you can become a trumpet medium, but it will cost you one thousand dollars cash. And you must swear never to reveal the secret."

The mark rushed out to the bank and came back with the money. Homer took the one thousand dollars and said to him, "It's very simple, my good man. You simply pick up the trumpet, push in the one end, and hold it in the air with your hand, and that's the way you do it!"

The sucker went into hysterics and fled the campground. Nobody ever saw him again.

Where money is concerned, I doubt if mediums would stop at anything, not excluding grave-robbing. In fact, I once took part in the equivalent of that.

An elderly man named Fred owned a house near Camp Chesterfield. One afternoon he was found dead in the house. The place was ramshackle and dreary and after dark looked exactly what a haunted house should look like.

It was said among the mediums that Fred had a lot of money stashed away around the place. The night of his death four of us—Raoul and I and two woman mediums—decided to search the house for the rumored loot. We started out from the camp on foot.

One of the women had the creeps. She was, like many mediums I knew, petrified of corpses, and the thought that we would be going into a house where one had lain so recently gave her goosebumps.

Suddenly a voice came out of the darkness. It turned out to be an inoffensive old lady inquiring where we four strangers, stumbling along in the dark, were going. However, at the sound of the voice the woman medium fainted dead away. And I mean dead—it took us ten minutes of slapping her wrists and fanning her to bring her around.

We finally got to the house, searched it for two hours, and left with three diamond pieces and almost $23,000 in cash that had been hidden in nooks and corners by the senile recluse. On the way back to the camp we split the proceeds and laughed about big, brave mediums who were afraid of the dark!

One medium searched a client's house immediately after her sudden death and found almost $50,000 in cash and several passbooks for bank accounts totaling more than $300,000.

The medium called the client's heir, saying that she had an urgent message from the deceased. In the message the medium revealed the locations, numbers, and totals of the bank accounts shown by the pass books she had confiscated. The heir was deeply grateful, and the medium was well rewarded for her trouble—a matter which had been stressed in the spirit message.

In later sittings various securities which the medium had lifted from the client's home during her search were "apported" to the heir, again with generous rewards for the medium.

The easiest money a medium can make—and it's been done countless times—is to offer "astral development lessons" for a fee ranging as high as one thousand dollars. (I know of such cases and it's not unreasonable to think that, if the traffic bore it, the fee has been even higher.)

The incredible gimmick here is that the astral lessons take place while the client is asleep! The medium's spirit guides promise to minister to him or her in the sleep state when the astral self is opened up to such instruction.

Nothing is required of the medium. He can be in a nightclub, on the beach, or drunk when the astral lessons are going on.

In order to get the money we did, we needed a congregation made up largely, if not wholly, of people at a certain financial level. We weren't interested in the very poor (though, curiously, later in my mediumship when my conscience began to prick me I actually gave some charity séances for sitters who couldn't pay—a sentimentality for which my fellow mediums roundly criticized me). To attract the right people, we had to give the church some class. And we did. We *did.*

When the congregation moved out of the temporary quarters we had occupied for two years or so into our own edifice, we renamed it the New Age Assembly Church and decided it was going to be first-class all the way. The investment, we knew, would pay off.

The church, though small (it seated about 250), was a showplace. The décor and appointments were, I think superb.

In the sanctuary we had eight imported crystal chandeliers, original oils hanging on the rear walls, and solid mirrors along the side interspersed with gilt columns. The columns were reproductions of antique design and very ornate. Two large Dresden urns sat in the front of the sanctuary. They had been acquired from the estate of William Randolph Hearst and were insured for $25,000.

In the foyer was a tremendous crystal chandelier, rare tapestries, oil paintings, and Regency period furniture.

The church was magnificently carpeted throughout.

The musical instruments were of high quality. There were two grand pianos, a spinet piano, and a Hammond concert organ with chimes. There were also Lyon and Healey concert harps. During the services all these instruments would accompany the congregational singing. The music was heavenly even if the spirit phenomena weren't. We created an atmosphere in which the dead could return in style.

Those who took part in the work of the church were in style too. All the hostesses, ushers, and those who greeted people at the door before a service wore formal dress. You didn't see much costume jewelry in our congregation; most of it was the real stuff. The atmosphere, though perhaps a bit overdone, created an aura of success, elegance, and glamour that attracted the rich, the fashionable, and the socially prominent. And we had more than our share of these types in the church.

Our Sunday evening services, which introduced most newcomers to the church, were quasireligious spectacles, theatrical productions, orchestrated by me to maximum effect. The idea was to hook the newcomer's interest to bring him back again. Eventually he would become one of the true believers who felt a pride in belonging to such a church and—the name of the game—*gave freely.*

The church became well-known. Once I took a cab there, and when I gave the destination, the driver looked at me and said, "New Age Assembly? My God, do you go to that church? I hear that the offering plates just float down the aisle!" I simply stared at him and said, "Yes, I go there, and that's true."

Just before I left the mediumship racket, plans were on the drawing board for a dream church which was to be a fitting monument to my career—as far beyond what I had then accomplished, as St. Peter's Basilica is beyond an obscure parish church. It was to be called the New Age Temple.

The plans were to build a palatial edifice with large Corinthian columns, a circular drive in front where arriving guests would be greeted by uniformed footmen, and valet parking for cars.

The church was to house a collection of fine art. Many of these items had already been selected—we were looking for others—including a few from some of the world's great estates.

An artist had been commissioned to create twelve oil paintings each twelve feet high and eight feet wide. The first of these had been completed and was in storage; it depicted the finding of Moses in the bulrushes.

In the sanctuary we planned as a backdrop to the platform a painting of the solar system on sliding panels, a curtain of gold lame, and behind both, gold pipes for the organ (to which $25,000 already had been pledged as a memorial). These would provide a kaleidoscope of backdrop effects since the lighting was to include changing colors on the draperies, the painting, and the organ pipes.

Twin pianos were to be on a revolving platform to one side of the main platform, the console of the pipe organ on the other side, behind which was to be seated a choral group or a small orchestra.

Eight tremendous crystal chandeliers had been purchased and were also in storage; these were to illumine the main sanctuary. Red velvet theater seats were to be placed in the sanctuary. A projection room was planned as part of the balcony, which would be used for special lighting, recording, and broadcasting.

Behind the main sanctuary was to be an enormous formal dining room with special lighting, candelabra, fine china, crystal, silver, linens, and art objects.

The New Age Ranch property and the property upon which the New Age Temple was to be erected could be seen from Florida's interstate highway. Two billboards were envisaged that would be seen by motorists using the highway. They were to read: NEW AGE TEMPLE—WHERE MIRACLES ABOUND! THE RELIGION OF THE NEW AGE PRESENTED IN AN OLD WORLD ATMOSPHERE! A crystal chandelier was to be our trademark.

The cost was to be enormous, of course, but the money was available—and much more. In fact, I expected the new temple, and particularly some of the innovations built around it, to send our income to the sky.

My master stroke was a plan to exploit to the fullest the desire—the *need*—most people have to be somebody; to rise above the drabness of their day-to-day existence; to experience a touch of glamour, excitement, drama, and high and unique honor.

We were going to confer on special contributors to the New Age Temple *titles of nobility*: Lord and Lady, Prince and Princess, Duke and Duchess. These honorifics, similar to papal titles, if you like, were to derive their distinction partly from the social status we expected the church to have in the community, but more distinction from the fact that they were to be conferred on the express instructions of the great Master Teachers from the exalted spirit planes. Besides elevating the titles beyond mere human honors, this would also let us, the mediums, off the hook when it came to explaining why this member was a Prince while another was merely a Lord.

There were to be rites of investiture in the church laden with pomp and pageantry and solemn mumbo-jumbo. Each title would carry with it distinctive medals and ribbons to be worn at special social functions.

I got the idea for all this partly from Father Divine's love feasts and partly from the titles of nobility dreamed up by another black messiah in Detroit a few years ago, Prophet Jones. But the final embellishments were to be my own.

My innovation would have been a gold mine. And the other mediums would have hated me even more, because they had lacked the imagination to do it first. But when they realized how it brought in the money, they would have borrowed the idea.

Most mediums come to tragic, tawdry ends, but they rarely die poor. . . .

M. Lamar Keene seated in the chair he used on the platform and for some trance sessions.

(top) Art Gallery, Camp Chester-
field   (right) 'Cathedral of the
Woods'; Camp Chesterfield
(bottom) The trail of religion,
Camp Chesterfield, Chesterfield,
Indiana

(top) Mother Simpson and Mabel   (bottom left) A typical "spirit photograph"   (bottom right) Two of the many homes occupied by mediums at Camp Chesterfield

Camp Silver Belle

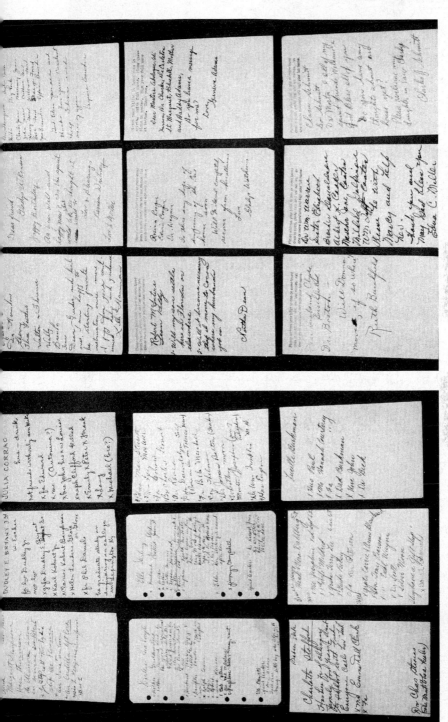

(left) Mediums' file cards written by psychics M. Lamar Keene worked with during his career. (right) Billets from a "billet file." These were written by the individuals who signed them.

(left) This is an invoice for apports. This investment would net at least $1,200.00, as indicated by the number of pieces. (right) Cards from mediums' file giving detailed information on clients

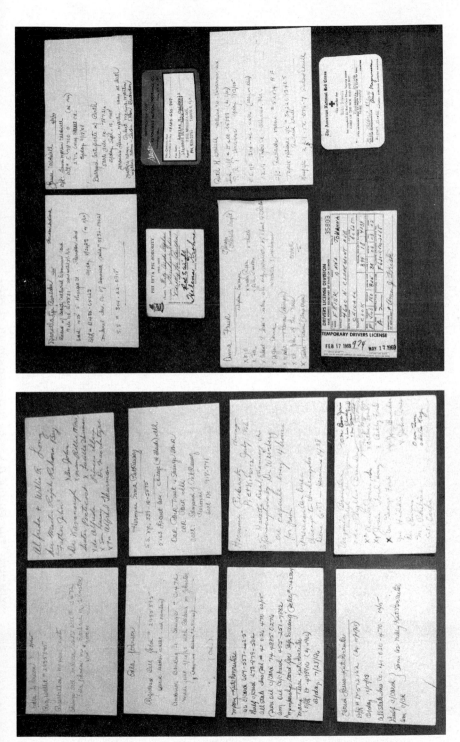

(left) More mediums' file cards   (right) Identification cards taken during seances to be apported at a future time during a public or private demonstration.

(left) A portion of the files taken by M. Lamar Keene when he left his church. (right) A letter received by M. Lamar Keene from a medium requesting that if anything should happen to her that her files are properly confiscated.

(top) Maxon Cafeteria, Camp Chesterfield, Chesterfield, Indiana. (right) Interior of 'Maxon' Cafeteria, Camp Chesterfield, Chesterfield, Indiana. (bottom) Bazaar, Camp Chesterfield, Chesterfield, Indiana.

Ethel Post Parrish

Ordination portrait of M. Lamar Keene. This was reproduced and sold at Camp Chesterfield as a post card.

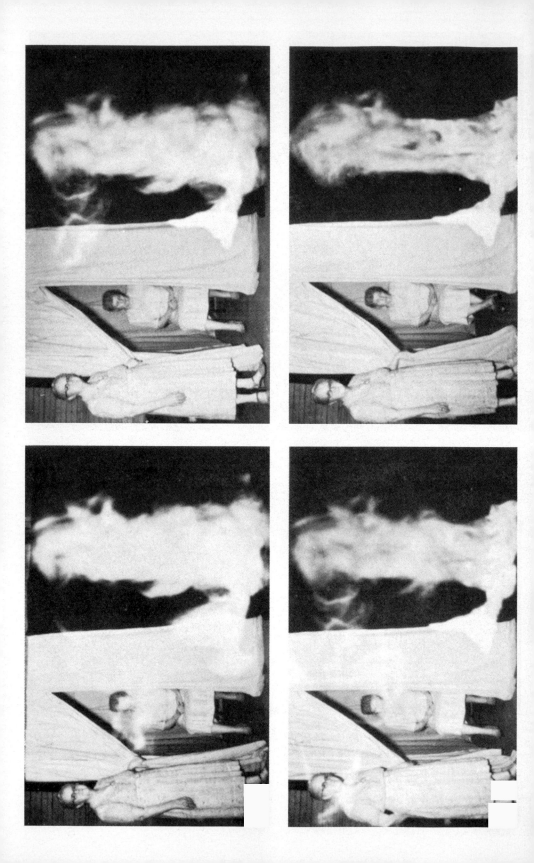

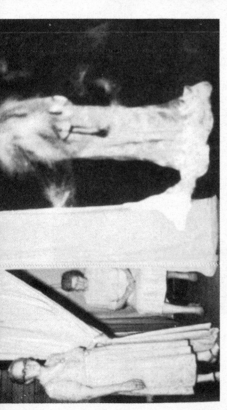

These curious photographs, featuring Ethel Post Parrish whom Lamar Keene describes as the "Queen Bee" of Camp Silver Belle, show the materialization of a spirit. The sequence of pictures depict the whole process of materialization (in this case, of Ethel Post Parrish's spirit guide, an Indian maiden named Silver Belle) from the first stage of vaporous, smoke-like ectoplasm to a fully formed, though two-dimensional figure. This series of photographs show what a sitter in the seance would think he had seen.

Of course, this is trick photography. One familiar method is to photograph smoke and then, by a double exposure, to superimpose on it either a drawing, or an actual accomplice dressed as a spirit, or a cardboard figure.

Needless to say, the woman to the left in the photograph, the "cabinet keeper," was an accomplice in the deception.

The one and only Mable Riffle

"Materialization" of spirit loved ones. Note the child spirit from in the front. Lamar Keene is dressed in the garb of his spirit guide.

My masonic friend William Twiss to whom in desperation I turned for help. He is examining pictures on silk called "precipatation."

5/SECRETS OF THE SEANCE, Or Giving the Spirits a Helping Hand

The source of all the gold, adulation, and sometimes fanatical devotion that surrounded me was the séance room and my prowess therein.

It was my inexplicable floating trumpet, through which the spirit communicators spoke with their families and friends still here on earth; my shimmering spirit forms, which not only spoke to the living but touched, even embraced them; my shatteringly accurate clairvoyance, which proved that the spirits followed the day-by-day existence of their loved ones, aware of the most trivial things in their lives—it was these mysterious psychic phenomena that kept the people coming and, most important, the money flowing in.

Oh, they liked the nice-nice sermons my partner and I preached. They enjoyed getting caught up in the rousing congregational singing. They reveled in the special music—the melodies of the piano, organ, and harp which spoke of comfort and hope. But what they really came for, *lived* for in many cases, were the spirit manifestations.

Take the séance room out of spiritualism and you re-duce it to another drab religion. That dark room, a mystic womb wherein unique wonders unfold, is to the spiritual-ist what baptism is to the Baptist, the Sabbath to the Sev-enth Day Adventist, or the cult of Mary to the traditionalist Roman Catholic. Central. The heart of the matter.

And so hundreds of people who waited upon my spirits for advice in marital, legal, medical, and other problems of their lives built their existence here and the hope of a fu-ture one hereafter on a mere magician's bag of tricks!

But what a bag of tricks! I've described some of the spec-tacular phenomena I created as the superdramatist of the séance room; now I'll tell you exactly how they were accomplished.

To get information on sitters, we had a variety of meth-ods, all devious. I've already mentioned pilfering purses and billfolds and picking pockets in the darkened séance room to dig out such data as social security numbers or bankbooks. We also made a rule that anyone wishing to be at a private or group séance had to attend three public church services beforehand. That way they could be ob-served and we could gather information on them from the billets they wrote. Each billet was stamped at the top: "Please address your billet to one or more loved ones in spirit, giving first and last names, ask one or more ques-tions and sign your full name." One billet thus made out gave us enough leads to come up with a file on anybody.

There were two small rooms on either side of the plat-form in the sanctuary, used only by the mediums, and these had two-way mirrors through which we could ob-serve the congregation before a service, determine who was there, and prepare our spirit messages accordingly. When a person got an evidential message he could always say to a skeptic, and no doubt often did, "The mediums didn't even see me before the service; if they need prior research for their messages, how could they have known to prepare one for me?" We made a point of knowing people better than they ever imagined we did.

Also, I had an electronic sound collector—a device for picking up sounds at a considerable distance—positioned in a house we owned across the street from the church. By aiming this at the church before a service, we harvested delicious bits of conversation that later were woven into startling messages.

My billet-reading, which was done with my eyes taped like a mummy's, I've already explained: I merely squinted down the side of my nose and read the billets by maneuvering them close to my body where I could catch a glimpse of them. Sounds childishly simple, perhaps, but it was a helluva impressive performance. I used to watch mentalists on television and in clubs and felt I needn't take a back seat to any of them.

Sometimes I read billets in sealed envelopes. Then, of course, I wore no blindfold; the problem here was to read the billet *through* the envelope. There were two methods popular among mediums, both of which I used.

One was to have a concealed light behind the pulpit against which the envelope could be held and which made it virtually transparent. The billet was of such a size that it fitted into the envelope without folding and thus could be read easily against the light.

Another method employed lighter fluid. Smeared on an opaque envelope, this makes it momentarily as transparent as cellophane. The fluid dries very quickly and leaves no detectable trace, so that the envelope could be returned to its original owner after the demonstration and proved to be still sealed and intact. Very impressive, especially when performed with dramatic flair.

Sometimes I would pull a dramatic variation on the standard billet-reading procedure. At the public sessions in the Cathedral at Camp Chesterfield, the billets normally were collected in a basket, carried to the pulpit, and hand-ed to the medium just as he started his demonstration. I had one of the workers (who was "open") filch a couple of billets before the demonstration and bring them to me be-hind stage. Then I prepared spectacular messages for the writers of those billets.

Later, as the basket containing the billets was being brought up the aisle in full view of the large congregation, I would dramatically exclaim, "Stop!" All eyes were upon me.

Even before donning my blindfold, I explained, the spirits were working and had told me the questions asked by two of those who had just written billets. I then pro-ceeded to quote the billets (and give appropriate answers) while they ostensibly were yet in the basket on which I hadn't placed a finger.

This was always the cue for a tremendous ovation, which I accepted with touching humility.

Of course, the evidential quality of my phenomena was cumulative; even if one performance—my blindfold billet-reading, say—wasn't in itself totally convincing to an individual, it tended to be accredited by the other pheno-mena which *were* convincing to him. If the sitter was con-vinced that I could materialize spirit forms, why should he think that I would need to stoop to cheating in any other phase of my mediumship? This line of reasoning served to strengthen any weak links in my chain of mediumistic per-formances.

Well, what about my utterly uncanny materializations? Stripped of the ectoplasm, here's what happened.

Let's move into the séance room for a typical reunion between the living and the dead. There was a semicircle of chairs in front of the "cabinet." The cabinet is a venerable institution in spiritualism, comparable to the baptismal font or the altar in other churches. It's simply a curtain drawn around an area, say eight feet by six feet, to make a closed-off cubicle; sometimes the curtain is simply drawn across the corner of the room.

The cabinet, according to the hifalutin' nonsense of spiritualism, serves as a kind of condensing chamber for the psychic force and ectoplasm (the mysterious substance drawn from the medium's body and the sitters') which enables the spirits to materialize. In actual fact, of course, it serves as a place where the medium can carry on his hanky-panky—get in and out of his gauzy spiritual raiment.

The sitters were invited to inspect the cabinet before the lights were turned out to see for themselves that there was no trap door or other secret entrance. (If there had been, and in many cases there are, the sitters won't find it.) In our séance room we had a hidden entrance, but not in the cabinet; it was in another part of the room and in the dark provided access for a confederate if he were needed.

Besides the cabinet, sitters were invited to inspect *me* to determine that I had nothing on my person to aid me in impersonating the spirits. Sometimes this search was performatory, sometimes more thorough.

When we were ready to proceed, I would enter the cabinet, in which was placed a single chair (or two if my partner and I were doing a double materialization sitting—this was supposed to provide more power), and draw the curtains. The lights were turned off except for one large red bulb controlled by a dimmer switch which cast enough glow to illumine the ectoplasm. Then the sitters sang a hymn.

For materialization sittings I wore black socks and pants which didn't show up at all in the dark. Then, while the sitters were singing, I would don my chiffon spirit garb. My outfit for a basic spirit (nothing fancy like a Master Teacher, who was "higher") resembled a baptismal robe. It

opened at the back to slip my arms into the sleeves, then
was secured by a simple snap. It covered everything from
the neck to the floor. I used various types of gauze headgear. When I was ready—which could be in as little as ten
seconds if necessary—I oozed from the cabinet, trailing
clouds of ectoplasm.

But how did I get my spirit raiment into the cabinet?
There were several ways.

Usually there is present at every materialization séance a
"cabinet attendant," who is actually the medium's bodyguard. Spiritualists explain his or her role as that of protecting the medium from malicious intruders who might
try to grab the ectoplasm and thereby cause the poor medium grave injury, even death. (Heartbreaking stories
were told to the faithful about mediums who had suffered
internal hemorrhages and writhed on the floor in agony
after some heartless knave grabbed their ectoplasm. The
official dogma was that rude touching of ectoplasm caused
it to recoil into the medium's body with savage force—like
being hit in the gut by a giant rubber band.) Anyway, the
cabinet attendant or keeper was there to discourage any
tampering with the ectoplasm—and also, in many cases, to
provide the ectoplasm.

Most cabinet attendants were women and carried large
handbags big enough to contain a hundred feet of tightly
packed chiffon. The stuff was simply passed to the medium inside the cabinet after the lights were turned out.

There were other methods. The average person has no
conception of how compressible chiffon is; enormous
quantities of it can be wadded into a ball small enough for
a man to hide in his undershorts. On occasion I was
searched down to my underwear and my contraband ectoplasm never found.

There are other, even less detectable ways of hiding it.

Some mediums have used body cavities. One woman medium told me her technique when she really wanted to confound some "smartassed investigator" was to stuff the chiffon into a condom and hide it in her vagina.

It's amazing what effects can be created in the dark manipulating yards and yards of chiffon and gauze which appears to shimmer in the unearthly glow of the ruby light. What I did was what magicians call "black art." The parts of me not covered by ectoplasm were garbed totally in black and were quite invisible in the dark. (For trumpet sittings, which I'll explain next, I wore a head-to-foot black outfit, including a mask over my face which rendered me as unseen as The Shadow used to be in his famous adventures.)

Standing in the séance room in my invisible outfit I would deftly unroll a ball of chiffon out to the middle of the floor and manipulate it until eventually it enveloped me. What the sitters saw was a phenomenon: A tiny ball of ectoplasm sending out shimmering tendrils which gradually grew or developed into a fully formed materialized spirit. Unless you have witnessed the effect under séance conditions you'll find it hard to grasp how eerily convincing it can be.

The ectoplasmic figure could disappear the same way it appeared. I simply unwound the chiffon from my body slowly and dramatically then wadded it back into the original tiny ball. What the sitter saw was the fully formed spirit gradually disintegrate, evaporate into a puff of ectoplasm.

The variations were endless. By standing in front of the cabinet and pulling the black curtains out and around me then manipulating them I could create the illusion of the spirit form *undulating*; varying in width from a mere inch to many inches; shooting from two feet to six feet in height (and if I stood on my toes considerably more) and then crumpling back to four feet, three, two, one . . . and through the floor. A whooshing sound added to the illusion of the form melting into the floorboards.

Often I combined astral music with the materializations. After one of the church musicians died I had recorded music of his harp-playing piped into the dark room and the sitters believed they were being serenaded by an angel.

One striking and very popular feature of our séances were astral duets played on the organ and piano (which were in the séance room and quite physical). Since Raoul, my partner, couldn't play anything but the radio it fell to me on such occasions to perform a duet solo. An interesting challenge!

I managed it by tape-recording organ music prior to the séance and then, in the pitch-darkness, accompanying the organ music live (or dead, if you like) on the piano. I introduced spontaneous little bits of business—such as interjected remarks—to demonstrate to the sitters that the piano actually was being played at that moment by a materialized spirit form and disarming suspicions that the whole thing was recorded.

I may be the only medium in history who regularly played piano-organ duets with himself!

We sometimes permitted infrared photographs to prove the reality of the materialization phenomena. These were snapped only when the spirits gave the signal guaranteeing that only what we wanted was captured on the film. Sometimes the photographs showed spirit forms, sometimes ectoplasm dribbling out of the medium's mouth or nose or ears while I lay slumped in my chair as though in trance.

With other mediums in black stealthily entering the room we could and at times did produce a host of materialized spirits—sort of an ectoplasmic convention. By myself I could produce other spirits by whirling around on the end of a stick a piece of chiffon sprayed with luminous paint. Coat hangers draped in ectoplasm also made a passable spirit, sort of half-materialized.

To portray a child I got down on my knees in the darkness. Sometimes sitters were invited to approach the spirit closely to peer directly into its face. I had a variety of face masks of men, women and children for all such occasions. These could be enormously convincing.

One medium at Camp Chesterfield was an enormous, grotesquely obese woman, yet in her materialization séances tiny spirit forms three or four feet tall skipped around the room, playfully touched the sitters, sometimes even climbed up on their laps and kissed them. Often there were three of these diminutive spirits visible at the same time.

This was amazing! But only to the sitter who didn't know that the medium, Martha Lomax, had three children and that there was a trapdoor in the floor of the séance room.

Besides being at home in my own well-equipped séance room, I was also a past master of the impromptu materialization. Give me any room, turn out the lights, and I'll produce spirit forms. My partner and I showed we could do it and do it well.

Once we conducted a materialization sitting at the home of an eccentric woman physician. There were fifteen sitters, whom we had insisted make reservations, so we were armed with plenty of research. Our cabinet from which the ectoplasmic forms were to emerge was simply a curtain flung over a wire across a corner of the living room.

My partner and I were both in a dangerous mood that night—bored with the standard effects and itching for some hellry—and we decided for fun to make the materializations out of our hostess's own items.

The way the cabinet was positioned, we had free access

out through the back of it to a nearby bedroom. We stripped the pillowcases and used them for ectoplasm. Later, the crazy doctor remarked on how much whiter and more dazzling the spirit forms had been than in previous materialization séances.

Of course, thumbing your nose at the sitter is a dangerous temptation for a medium, since it can make him careless. I tried never to under-estimate my sitter's intelligence even if he appeared the stupidest one I'd had yet.

In the house séance just mentioned, an incident occurred which showed how psychology can conquer dogma. I recognized two of the sitters as a mother and daughter. The daughter's husband, a fervent Pentecostal, was fanatically opposed to spiritualism as a thing of the Devil, and I knew that he had driven his wife and mother-in-law to our church in Tampa but sat outside in the car, refusing even to set foot in Satan's domain. Later we found that he had sought an injunction to prevent the séance in the doctor's house.

Anyway, I had one of the materalized spirits that night tell his wife, "Your husband is really a very fine man and you're fortunate to be married to him. Please tell him that!"

She did, and two weeks later he was in our church and soon became a member.

My real contribution to the science and art of mediumship was in creating an original trumpet phenomenon. The standard trumpet sitting takes place in the familiar darkness—sometimes with the red light, sometimes without—and voices heard speaking through the tin megaphone are said to be those of the spirits.

Some mediums just sit or stand in the darkness and talk through the trumpet, but these show little initiative or imagination. Our trumpets had a luminous band so that the sitters could see them whirling around the room, hovering in space, or sometimes swinging back and forth in rhythm with a hymn.

The trick was the old black art business. My partner and I, and other confederates if we needed them, wore head-to-toe black outfits which rendered us invisible in the darkness. We could handle the trumpet with impunity even in a good red light and with the luminescent bands giving off a considerable glow.

The trumpets, as I've mentioned earlier, were made in sections and were extendable to a total length of about four feet. Thus they could be swung around with considerable speed. The sitter, thinking the trumpet was only a foot long and seeing it whizzing around close to the ceiling, assumed that it had gotten up there by defying gravity.

Some skeptics, of course, suspected wires or threads, but my special trumpet effect really bamboozled them. It bamboozled everybody and may be justly described as one of the few truly original phenomena in mediumship.

The sitter's experience was of holding the trumpet in his or her hands and feeling it vibrate with voice sounds. Yet there were no wires, no cords—nothing.

We had one man at Camp Chesterfield who considered himself a skeptic and an expert on mediumistic tricks, but he couldn't fathom my vibrating trumpet. This man, in the darkened séance room lit by the glow of the ruby bulb, took the trumpet which had gently descended into his lap, put his hands on it, shook it, collapsed it, reassembled it, placed it under his chair—and still he could feel the tin quivering.

"My God," he said to his wife, "the voices are still coming out!"

At that, the Indian chief who was speaking through the trumpet boomed from under the chair, "Of course, you damned fool, what did you expect? I'm a spirit!"

Other mediums, including some big names in the spook business, offered me thousands of dollars for the secret. But the secret is so simple it eludes detection. This is how it was done.

I did not talk through the trumpet nestling on the sitter's knee but through another trumpet, painted black so as to be invisible in the dark. Dressed in my head-to-toe black outfit, I spoke in the dark through the black trumpet which I held a short distance—three or four feet—from the other trumpet in the sitter's lap. My voice, passing through the black trumpet and striking the other trumpet, caused it to vibrate. Try it for yourself!

We used to pull this stunt along with five or six other trumpets bouncing around in the air simultaneously. This added to the confusion, and before long sitters were going away and telling others that in our séances six trumpets spoke at the same time!

Of course, I would be dashing around the room in the dark, throwing my voice from here, there, and everywhere. The overall impression was of a fantastically evidential séance with trumpets talking to beat the band and the room jumping with psychic energy.

With experience I became as stealthy and nimble as a cat in the dark. Never once did I trip or stumble. Who knows—maybe I'm psychic?

It might have been fun sometime to match wits with a parapsychologist—a professional ghost-hunter. Our only experience with a self-styled parapsychologist—how valid was his claim to the title is doubtful—started when a young man presented himself at the church and said that he was affiliated with Dr. J. B. Rhine of Duke University, the high priest of ESP. He was intrigued by reports of our trumpet sittings, the young man told us, and he proposed a test in which the trumpet was to be coated with a special powder (the idea being, of course, that if we ourselves were manipulating the trumpet, telltale stains would stick to our fingers).

The first thing we did was to contact Rhine. We discovered that he had no knowledge of anybody by the name his alleged associate had given us. But Raoul and I decided it would be amusing to string the would-be scientist along. We agreed to his "test" séance.

Before the sitting the young investigator, with exemplary diligence, made a thorough search and satisfied himself that only he and I were in the séance room and that there was only one trumpet, which he proceeded to coat with his powder. Then the lights were turned off.

In a moment, spirit voices were heard from the trumpet, which performed its usual gyrations. The young investigator was shocked and embarrassed when the spirits told him that they were aware of his lie—that he was not associated with Dr. Rhine nor ever had been. Then they assured him that the results of his "test" would be a vindication of spiritualism.

After the lights came on, the incipient parapsychologist examined carefully both the trumpet and my hands. The powder on the trumpet was undisturbed, and there were no stains on my fingers.

The young man was shaken. He seemed to fear that he really had been tampering with some higher force!

How had I pulled off the trick?

Easily. I managed it without assistance from Raoul or another confederate. All I needed was another trumpet, or quasi trumpet, besides the one coated with the powder. So before the séance I rolled a large piece of pliable cardboard around my leg and held it in place by tucking it into the elasticized top of my sock.

Later, in the darkness of the séance, this piece of cardboard became a makeshift megaphone.

For all I know that zealous young investigator may have

written a technical report in some learned journal of parapsychology about his successful test.

An added attraction we sometimes offered in trumpet sittings was the levitation of the sitter. This was accomplished with the utmost ease.

The room was in total darkness. Raoul and I both worked out with weights and were very strong. So in our invisible black garb we simply took hold of the sitter's chair—made of sturdy steel—and lifted her into the air. To hoist a chair with a 130-pound woman sitting on it was for us no problem at all. As we each gripped two legs of the chair, it slowly rose in the air. We usually got it so high that the sitter could reach up and touch the ceiling.

Time after time we performed this stunt and the sitters were convinced they had been made to float by the same psychic power that made the trumpets airborne.

I was also a whiz at apports. These were gifts from the spirits: sometimes they were worthless trinkets like rings or brooches; other times, more impressively, they were (as I've already described) objects we had stolen from the sitter.

The apports, as previously described, sometimes arrived in full light and other times tumbled out of the trumpet in the dark. In exotic variations I arranged for apports to turn up in a newly baked cake, in a sandwich, or inside a shoe.

Once at a church function I told a woman the spirits had apported something for her into a chocolate cake, and when she cut into it and found her necklace, she screamed, "Oh my God, this was at home in my drawer when I left to come to church!"

The truth was that we had pilfered it from her purse more than a month before and she evidently hadn't missed it.

Some mediums apported only certain kinds of apports,

which they bought cheap in bulk. One woman specialized in silly little bits of colored glass—"spirit jewels." A male medium I know apported only arrowheads, which he dug up somewhere by the hundreds. I have invoices for large purchases of items such as costume jewelry that made good bread-and-butter apports. To special customers, however, I gave something more impressive.

My partner and I apported practically everything but a live cobra, and we might have gotten around to that eventually. Orchids, roses, plants of various shapes and sizes— these were common. Once I apported a huge thistle plant bristling with wicked thorns. Another time I apported a fresh, whole thistle plant, including the root, to every sitter at the séance. I also apported live animals—mice, gerbils, kittens—and Indian arrowheads by the hundreds.

The apports were smuggled into the room under cover of darkness by my black garbed confederate. The only one he really complained about handling was that giant thistle. He said the damn thing nearly pricked him to death!

Since the room was in total darkness the sitters were unaware of my confederate's coming and going and believed that the spirits had materialized the apports out of thin air.

Among my followers a favorite phenomenon was spirit card writing. Blank cards were given to each sitter, and he or she was asked to sign his or her name. The cards were then collected and placed on a table in the center of the room, and the lights were lowered. A hymn was sung, the lights were turned on, and *voilà*! the cards now bore spirit messages, signatures of dead loved ones, Bible verses, poems, personal reminiscences, and other heartwarming evidences of life after death.

There were two ways of doing this. The cards signed by the sitters could be removed from the room in the dark by confederates and the messages added, then returned before the lights were turned on. The other way was to have cards prepared in advance, including look-alike forgeries of the sitters' signatures, and simply switch these for the blank cards.

A variation was to have the spirits put on the cards the name and signature of the sitter's Master Teacher and a drawing of him. (Everybody who attended our séances eventually was assigned a Master Teacher: an exalted spirit being, wise, beneficent, and immensely powerful, who functioned more or less like the traditional guardian angel. People grew very attached to their Master Teachers and often prayed to them as Catholics do to the saints. Materializing them was fun. We didn't need to worry about evidential details—except to be careful not to have the great one contradict too blatantly something that he had said on a previous occasion—and we could deck ourselves out with beards, headgear, jewels, and other fancy trappings of an astral VIP.)

Occasionally, just for variety and a different kind of challenge, I would do spirit precipitation on silk. It was a good seller because it gave the sitter something to take away with him as a tangible token of spirit power.

The sitters were each given a piece of silk before the séance started. They were told to hold these and meditate on the spirits to try to attune themselves to the etheric vibrations. Then all placed their pieces of silk on a table in the center of the room, and the lights were dimmed.

When the lights came back on, after ten, twenty, or thirty minutes of hymn-singing, each of the pieces of silk bore a spirit image. Sometimes the face would be that of a loved one, often that of an unidentified spirit who, we explained, must have some deep psychic affinity with the sitter.

The trick here was to prepare the silks in advance. I used to cut pictures out of old magazines or use snapshots of spirits known to the sitters if I had them, soak the picture in ammonia for thirty seconds, place it on bridal silk, put a handkerchief over it, and use a hot iron. The image impregnated the silk.

Sometimes, to anticipate suspicion or skepticism, I would have the sitters sign their pieces of silk, then have those removed in the dark by confederates who did the impregnating of the images in an adjacent room and returned the silks before the end of the séance.

Actually, we found that bridal satin took the pictures better and was easier to iron but we still called it spirit precipitation on silk.

Once at Camp Chesterfield, while doing precipitations, I got lazy or careless or both and caused a minor crisis. Sick of cutting out and ironing the damn things, I used any picture that was handy, one of a little girl on a recent cover of *Life* magazine. The woman who got the silk recognized the picture and went to Mamie Schultz Brown, the president of the camp that year. Mamie was very excitable; she almost fainted when the woman confronted her with the silk and the incriminating picture from *Life*.

However, we smoothed it over by telling the woman that sometimes the spirits did mischievous things like that just to remind us they were still human and liked a joke.

One of the garden-variety miracles we purveyed that required no paraphernalia was predicting the future. Our prophecies were based on logic, reasonable inference from known facts, and common sense. Sometimes, just for the hell of it, we would take an absolutely wild guess and come up with a zinger.

We constantly made predictions for people about their personal lives. And annually, just after the new year, we had a sort of gala prediction party where the spirits gave a glimpse of coming political and world events. We had maybe a hundred people at five dollars a head turn out to hear this preview of the news.

We always gave ourselves an out, of course, in the event

that the prophecy didn't materialize. The "vibrations" had changed, we would say, or people's prayers had averted the gloom and doom that we had warned about but that hadn't come to pass.

Actually, our track record as prophets wasn't bad. We predicted that John Kennedy would be elected president. The year that California had a really bad fire, we had predicted bad fires in that state. We even called one of the California earthquakes several months before it happened.

One medium I knew, based in Washington, D.C., specialized in political predictions and often was very astute. There was at least one senator among his sitters and I'm sure he had other excellent contacts with the Washington grapevine.

I was very good at predicting events for individuals. Some of them almost surprised me.

I warned one woman in the church that her children would try to tie up her financial assets and railroad her into a rest home. This would happen, I said, after her husband's death.

Well, her husband did predecease her; sure enough, her son, a doctor, tied up everything financially, and the woman is now in a rest home in Florida. These developments I predicted seven years before the event.

What about horse races, lotteries, and football games?

My standard reply when people asked me to predict these, and they did, was that my concern was with spiritual things and not crass materialism.

One woman came to a séance and, when the lights were out, asked to speak to her Master Teacher. She said, "I want to go to Las Vegas and I want you to give me some numbers to play. When I return I'll give half of everything I win to the church."

Master Teacher replied, "Well, I have a better idea. Why don't I give the medium the numbers and let him go to Las

Vegas; when he returns, he can give *all* the winnings to the church!"

One thing I haven't explained is my eating glass in front of the congregation without killing myself. In the first chapter I described how I emptied a glass of water over some flowers, wrapped the glass in a handkerchief, broke it, and munched on the pieces—while the congregation bellowed a hymn. Actually, some of them were too shocked to sing. I thought my poor uninitiated mother would have a stroke! But, of course, I was unharmed because I was protected by spirit power.

What really protected me was that before the service I had placed a dish containing ice inside the pulpit. What I crunched with such obscene gusto (right into the microphone, so that it sounded as though I was devouring the whole water-glass) was a piece of ice.

Not all mediums were as adept as I was.

In December, 1974, William Rauscher and Allen Spraggett visited The Peoples' Spiritualist Church in St. Petersburg. That night, the pastor, the Rev. Mamie Schultz Brown was doing billet-reading. It was such a blatant imposture that the aged medium, unable to use a blindfold because she can't see without her thick glasses, didn't make even a pretence of covering her eyes. She just went through the billets, opening them more or less surreptitiously (though what she was doing should have been obvious to a wide-awake 10-year-old) and reading the question. Then she gave stock answers.

Bill Rauscher submitted a billet with a phony question: "Will my Uncle Sherwood's estate be settled by the end of the month?" Needless to say, Bill Rauscher has not, nor ever has had, an Uncle Sherwood, incarnate or discarnate.

The medium's answer to this planted question showed both her total lack of ESP and her semi-literacy.

"Yes, your Uncle Sherwood's estate will be settled in a

month," the medium intoned. "Also, I just seen much blessings around you. And your Uncle Sherwood is saying, 'I didn't mean no harm? What I sometimes said didn't mean nothin'.' Do you understand what your uncle means?"

Bill Rauscher nodded gravely that he did and the medium smiled at another customer she had conned (or so she thought).

Many of the wonders I purveyed I created myself. But later, after leaving mediumship, I discovered that there actually had been many precedents. The motley crew at Camp Chesterfield, and my phony spirits, are nothing new to spiritualism.

No, nothing new at all. . . .

6/A SHORT HISTORY OF MEDIUMISTIC FRAUD, or "Spooks-a No Come"

How did modern spiritualism—a movement whose philosophy is on the whole more sensible than that of many religions—come to be infested with fraud?

Is wholesale spiritualist fraud exclusively a contemporary phenomenon? A freakish departure from a past purity of faith? An aberration?

Is it an accident of history? Did spiritualism in the United States just happen to fall into the hands of a bunch of amoral adventurers who perverted it to their own use—as the papacy fell into the hands of the Borgias and Medicis and other unsavory types?

Well, it would be comforting perhaps to be able to take this view, but it doesn't fit the facts. The facts are that from its very beginning modern spiritualism has been riddled with fakery, humbug, and deceit.

Let's take a look at this bitter legacy, which has borne its rankest fruit in our day.

It started with the founders of modern spiritualism, Kate and Maggie Fox, who as young girls in their home near Rochester, New York, began experiencing strange

115

raps that were said to come from spirits. Many groups, including scientific committees, investigated the Fox sisters and their spirit raps and were baffled. One committee, which included the famous author Horace ("Go West, young man") Greeley, concluded that "whatever may be the origin or cause of the rappings, the ladies in whose presence they occur do not make them."

Then in 1888 both sisters confessed that the raps were a hoax produced by cracking their toe-joints. This explanation already had occurred to some skeptics, but nobody had been able to produce raps as convincing as those of the Fox sisters. After her confession, Margaret, in a demonstration at New York's Academy of Music, showed exactly how she had bamboozled scientists. Standing on a little pine table on the stage, wearing nothing on her feet but stockings, the co-mother of modern spiritualism caused raps to be heard throughout the auditorium.

"As she remained motionless," said a contemporary account, "loud distinct rappings were heard—now behind the scenes on stage, now in the gallery."

The varying locations of the raps were actually a trick of acoustics (something Maggie and her sister had often relied upon). The sounds all came from the medium's feet and were caused by her snapping the joint of her big toe.

"I began the deception when I was too young to know right from wrong," Maggie told the audience on that occasion.

(It should be noted that later Maggie and Kate Fox repudiated their confessions and said they had been bribed to make them by enemies of spiritualism. But so far as I'm concerned, and many others, the confessions are too damning to be explained away.)

Materializations of spirits developed early in the history of modern spiritualism, sometime during the 1860s, it seems. And one of the first mediums to produce full-form materializations (in which, of course, I specialized) was none other than Leah Fish Underhill, née Fox—younger sister of Kate and Maggie. Nothing like keeping fraud in the family.

Two of the brightest stars of early spiritualism and, by the way, the inventors of the "spirit cabinet"—that sanctuary within which, free from prying eyes, the physical medium can prepare his tricks—were the Davenport Brothers, Ira and William.

They were securely tied with ropes and bound hand and foot, and the doors of their cabinet were shut. Almost immediately it was hellzapoppin'. Musical instruments played, bells rang, and hands appeared at the windows of the cabinet. Yet when the doors were opened a moment later, the Davenports were firmly tied, and the handfuls of salt placed in their clenched fists as a test were still there.

The brothers never claimed to be spiritualists, but on the other hand they didn't go out of their way to discourage the idea, either. They just let audiences make up their own minds; meanwhile, the shekels rolled in. Now we know that to stage their supernatural shenanigans the Davenports employed as many as ten confederates at one time.

It wasn't only in the United States, spiritualism's native land, that fraud abounded. The new movement had spread early to Britain, where it attracted a relatively strong following among the educated middle-class. But before long British mediums were being caught red-handed in chicanery, just like their American counterparts.

The most famous of materialization mediums, Florence Cook—though she managed to convince a scientist, Sir William Crookes, that she was genuine—was repeatedly exposed in fraud. Florence had been trained in the arts of the séance by Frank Herne, a well-known physical medium whose materializations were grabbed on more than one occasion and found to be the medium himself.

Another Victorian medium, Mrs. Guppy, specializing in apports, delighted in bringing her sitters fresh fruits, vegetables, and flowers (remember my thistle plants?). On one occasion Mrs. Guppy claimed to have been "teleported" across London a distance of three miles and dropped down through the ceiling of a room smack into the middle of a séance—all without a scratch, of course. Hmmm.

William Eglinton was a celebrated English physical medium who produced not only materializations but also—a new twist—self-levitations. Eglinton's own body, it was said, became buoyant and rose into the air, sometimes as high as the ceiling. Always in the dark, of course.

Eglinton was exposed so often it must have gotten boring. On one occasion a false beard and a quantity of muslin were found in his trunk by an investigator, Archdeacon Colley. Nobody except spiritualists believed that the medium was simply getting ready for a masquerade party.

In 1880 another famous medium, Madame D'Esperance, was exposed—literally. Ectoplasm grabbed in the dark by a sitter turned out to be the medium in total deshabille. After that embarrassing interlude, Madame D'Esperance apparently became more careful since she wasn't busted again for thirteen years.

Such a series of exposures shook the faith even of spiritualists, and by the turn of the century physical mediumship, once the movement's glory and wonder, had declined to the point of virtual extinction. Then, like the flu that always seems to come back worse than before, physical mediumship revived.

In the early part of this century and into the 1920s and to an extent the 1930s, spiritualism enjoyed a new vogue, and with it the mediums who could float tables and make trumpets talk and ghosts walk. The law of supply and demand wrought its inevitable result: mediums suddenly rediscovered physical phenomena.

One of the biggest stars was a semiliterate Neapolitan woman, Eusapia Palladino, whose spirit hands and levitations were exposed so often as tricks that they would hardly be remembered if the medium hadn't also had a fantastic ability to bounce back. No sooner had she been debunked by one committee than she returned bigger and bolder than ever, with a new army of convinced believers, including psychical researchers, traipsing along behind her.

In 1910, after being exposed and rehabilitated a dozen times by different committees, Eusapia gave six sittings in New York. At first the phenomena were wonderful. In the dark the table lifted, bells rang, raps and thumps were heard. However, unknown to the medium, two spies dressed in black crept into the room after the lights were out, crawled along the floor, and saw her tip the table with her toe, ring the bell with a free hand which she had wriggled loose from control, and produce the bangs with her hands and feet.

Palladino never tried another comeback. Maybe she was too old or too tired. Anyway, she returned to sunny Naples and spent the rest of her life presumably making spaghetti instead of wonders.

However, Eusapia returned after her death, appropriately enough, through another Neapolitan medium, one Nino Pecoraro, who claimed the great Palladino as his spirit guide.

In 1922 Pecoraro gave a sitting in New York for Sir Arthur Conan Doyle and his wife in which objects flew around and the voice of the deceased Eusapia offered spir-

it greetings. Sir Arthur, a spiritualist who believed everything, was impressed because during the séance Pecoraro
had been securely tied to a chair with picture wire, he said.

Well, Houdini, who was then ghost-busting, rushed into
the fray and challenged Pecoraro to produce phenomena
after he, Houdini, had gotten through tying him. The
young medium unwisely agreed.

This time the tying was done with short pieces of fish
line, and Houdini supervised it. When the lights were
turned out, the sitters waited for the spirits to come . . .
and waited . . . and waited. . . .

Finally, the apologetic voice of the medium was heard
from the cabinet, uttering the words for which he became
famous: "Spooks-a no come."

Exit Nino Pecoraro.

During the late 1920s and the 1930s, one of the stars of
spiritualism was an unusual woman called by some the
Blonde Witch of Boston, and by others "the most beautiful
medium in the world." Her name: Mina Crandon, alias
Margery the Medium.

Margery produced just about everything: apports; globs
of ectoplasm, some of which looked like hands; spirit
lights; spirit voices; and automatic writing. Her spirit
guide was a deceased brother, Walter Stinson, who had an
undisguised hostility toward skeptics.

"Houdini, you goddamned sonofabitch, get out of
here!" was the way Walter greeted the famous magician,
accusing him of trying to frame the medium.

In Margery's séances, sitters often felt the touch of spirit
fingers light as a cobweb. Once the wooden cabinet she was
in broke apart under the violent force of the psychic energy. And on another occasion a live pigeon was apported
fluttering into the locked séance room. Spectacular stuff!

Many investigators, such as Professor William McDou-
gall and J. B. Rhine, said Margery was fraudulent and sug-

gested ways in which she probably produced her effects. But nobody ever quite caught her in the act of cheating.

The worst blow to Margery's mediumship came after she began demonstrating a new type of phenomenon: the formation of imprints in dental wax of the thumb of her spirit guide, Walter. These thumbprints were quite unlike those of the medium. What was eventually established, however, was that they matched exactly those of a friend of Margery, a dentist named Kerwin who was very much alive. It was he who first suggested the use of dental wax to obtain such spirit thumbprints.

Later, a scientist showed that from a given set of fingerprints it is not difficult to make dies by which the prints can be transferred to any object.

When Margery was on her deathbed, psychical researcher Nandor Fodor asked her to set the record straight. How did she produce her amazing pheonomena?

Raising herself from the pillow, she muttered, "Go to hell. All you psychic researchers can go to hell.

"Why don't you guess how I did it? You'll all be guessing . . . for the rest of your lives."

Spoken like a true medium. . . .

Today mediumistic chicanery isn't confined to the citronella circuit of American spiritualist camps or down-at-the-heels storefront churches. It exists, as you have seen from my own story, in posh churches attended by well-to-do people. And it still goes on in Britain, as here, just as it did in Victorian times.

One of the slickest recent operators in British spiritualism was a character named William Roy who in 1958, when his exposure as a fraud was imminent, sold his confessions to the London *Sunday Pictorial* for a tidy sum. (It should be noted that in this case the exposure was instigated by sincere spiritualists, chiefly Maurice Barbanell, then editor of the periodical *Two Worlds*.)

Roy was a cunning customer who, judging by the accounts, might have made a good partner for me in my heyday. He specialized in "direct voice," by which the spirits spoke with or without a trumpet. He also went in for materializations on a grand scale, including those of such personages as Gandhi, Napoleon, and apparently even Christ. Like me, he majored in evidential messages which stunned with their accuracy.

And like me, Roy, as revealed in his confessions, kept card index files on sitters, went through their purses and billfolds to get useful information, and bugged pre-séance conversations to pick up juicy tidbits. In addition, he used the standard gimmicks of the physical medium: the chiffon ectoplasm, the reaching-rods to manipulate the trumpets in the dark, and the black-garbed confederates in the séance room.

The sequel to Roy's story is significant. And depressing. After a period of exile abroad, this self-confessed fraud returned to Britain and, according to reports, resumed his mediumship under another name. Some of those who frequent his séances apparently know his past but prefer to believe that he once had genuine powers, lost them through faking, but now has recovered them.

There *is* a will to believe. . . .

A medium still riding high in England is Leslie Flint, famed as an exponent of direct voice. William Rauscher and Allen Spraggett, who attended a sitting Flint held in 1970 in New York, told me that it was the most abysmal flop of any séance they had endured. All the spirit voices sounded exactly like the medium and displayed an incredible ignorance of nearly everything pertaining to the sitters. The "mediumship" was second-rate ventriloquism.

A medium who died not too long ago was one of the most colorful and successful necromancers in the United States. His name was Frank Decker, and he was a friend not only of Arthur Ford, the famed psychic, but also of Joseph Dunninger, the master mentalist.

In 1932 Decker accomplished a coup which many mediums have dreamed about but never succeeded in bringing off: he passed a test imposed by a magician. Or at least he said he did.

At the séance in question, attended by twenty-four sitters, one of them announced himself as M. Taylor of 1427 Broadway, a member of the Society of American Magicians, and said that he had come to issue a challenge to the medium. Producing a brand-new United States mail sack, Mr. Taylor challenged Frank Decker to perform spirit phenomena while locked inside it. The medium accepted the challenge and stepped into the mail bag. It was drawn up over his head, fastened, and locked. The lights in the room were then turned out.

Almost immediately Patsy, the medium's spirit guide, cheerfully declared that the medium was okay and that if the magician would promise to let Decker keep the mailbag as a memento, the spirits would release him posthaste. Mr. Taylor gladly complied with the request.

Within twenty minutes the mailbag dropped on the magician's lap, as though deposited there by the spirits. When the lights were turned on the medium was still in a trance, sprawled on the floor.

Later, examination revealed that the lock on the mailbag was intact, showing no evidence of having been tampered with.

The story of Decker's triumph over the magician made sensational news in spiritualist journals and was soon repeated in a book by a physician, Dr. E. F. Bowers. However, Dr. Bowers was forced to delete the reference to the incident from his book under threat of a lawsuit by the Society of American Magicians. The magicians had investigated and found that they had no member named M. Tay-

lor nor had anyone of that name resided at the address
given in Decker's account.

However, Martin Sunshine, a magic dealer at that same
address, gave the Society of American Magicians an affida-
vit declaring that he had sold Frank Decker a trick mailbag, such as stage escapologists use, and had acted as the
medium's confederate by pretending to be M. Taylor, a
magician.

Sometimes, a phony medium goes too far and is caught
by the sincere spiritualists themselves. These confronta-
tions can be colorful to say the least.

Here's an account of such an exposure of a fraudulent
medium, described in an open letter to interested parties
by the Reverend Frances Converso, president of the Temple of Wisdom Church, Baltimore, and its vice-president,
the Reverend Walter Sutton.

"We regret," says the statement, "that such an incident
as occurred at Camp Boynton on Memorial Day was
caused by the trickery and deception of someone associated with the Church.

"In order to expose this fraudulence, responsible members of the congregation found it necessary to obtain the
help of the detectives present that night, May 30, 1969.

"Pictures were taken and many individuals present at
that time were able to see Mr. White wrapped in cloth at
what purported to be an Outdoor Materialization of 'Red
Feather,' an Indian Spirit. Mr. White had announced that
the materialization would consist of 'ectoplasm' manifest-
ing by drawing it from the medium but not motivated by
his own physical body.

"At the time of exposure Mr. White [supposed to be in
trance] ran shoeless a couple of hundred feet into the
woods. Rev. Sutton saw what was transpiring and pursued
him.

"As Reverend Sutton approached Mr. White [minus

robe] came out of the thicket. Reverend Sutton escorted Mr. White back to the rock where the Materialization was held, voicing to him and the congregation the fakery, until he was set upon by a few individuals.

"In the company of a witness Reverend Sutton went to where Mr. White came out of the thicket and found glossy white robes and an Indian head dress attire. Seeing this, Mr. White tried to retrieve the 'costume.' Reverend Sutton avoided his tackle and proceeded down the hill displaying the costume to those still gathered there. Some of Mr. White's friends and a couple of misinformed individuals threw Reverend Sutton to the ground and managed to rend most of the costume from him.

"Shortly thereafter, Mr. White ordered the costume, which he belatedly claimed was 'planted' in the woods [at the spot to which he ran] to be burned, thus destroying this portion of the evidence.

"The above account has been attested by numerous individuals present who have volunteered to be witnesses in this matter.

"We wish malice to none but the Temple of Wisdom cannot and shall not tolerate acts of deceit by anyone under the auspices of said Church; realizing fully that this incident is a deplorable reflection upon us, we hope that no one becomes disillusioned but that all will continue to pursue Truth and the benefits of our religion."

The last I heard, "Red Feather" was slinging hash in a diner in Ocean City, N.J.

Don't knock it. It's an *honest* living. . . .

A never-before-told episode in which a phony materialization and trumpet medium was unmasked involved the late controversial Bishop James Pike.

Pike, an ecclesiastical maverick whose sensational heresy near-trials won him headlines, also attracted world attention when he went on television with the late medium Arthur Ford and became convinced that he had talked with his dead son.

That Ford cheated in that séance, by doing extensive prior research, was eventually discovered by Canon William Rauscher and Allen Spraggett, who published the facts in their biography of Ford. In the light of a forthcoming biography of Pike (which, by the way, exposes some pretty explosive facts about his private life, as well as going into great detail about who may have duped him about the psychic before Ford did—the biographers suggest it was his former secretary) this hitherto unrevealed episode takes on added interest.

The facts, as recalled by Allen Spraggett who was there, are these: In February 1968 Bishop Pike and several other people had a series of séances with a medium from Southern California. He said he could produce materialized spirit forms, and spirit voices from a trumpet under test conditions.

The sittings—there were four—took place over a two-day period in a hotel room in Santa Barbara. The group included, besides Pike, his then secretary [later wife] Diane Kennedy, Dr. Ian Stevenson, then head of the department of psychiatry at the University of Virginia Medical School [a respected parapsychologist], and Allen Spraggett and his wife Marion.

The medium reneged on his promise to perform under "test" conditions by permitting only an excruciatingly dim red light in the pitch-black séance room [instead of the bright one agreed upon] and refusing to allow infrared photographs of the materialized forms. He said that if the group was satisfied with the initial manifestations the spirits would permit more freedom at later séances.

Anyway, from the accounts, he was a real artist.

A big, tall he-man looking type [appearances can be deceptive] he was accompanied by his inevitable cabinet attendant [read, accomplice], a matronly, rotund woman who wore a hat like a potted plant and a fake fox fur wrap.

The medium rigged up a cabinet by stringing a black curtain across a corner of the hotel room, sat inside it and the curtain was drawn and the lights turned out.

In a few moments what looked like streams of luminous, almost vaporous substance extruded from under the curtain, ebbing and flowing. Then a whirling column of "ectoplasm" formed and reached a height of more than six feet. It undulated, pulsing as though alive and varying from a few inches across at times to three or four feet. Then it dwindled and seemed to sink through the floor.

The guy was good, no doubt about it, and the sitters were intrigued. Then followed a procession of forms—from a giant Indian named Shimmering Leaf to a three-foot idiot child spirit named Ivy [with a face which Diane Kennedy examined from only a few inches away and said looked amazingly human].

Later the group of sitters—somewhat less credulous than the usual breed—conducted an inquest on the séance.

Marion Spraggett, who had a good vantage point because she sat at right angles to the cabinet [a mistake on the medium's part] was able to confirm the others' suspicions that the undulating forms were produced by the medium manipulating the curtains. The child figure with a face was, they decided, the medium on his knees [draped in chiffon of course] and wearing a mask.

The medium was careless. One sitter spotted that the pig-tails of the Indian spirit were identical to the long stringy moustache of an Eastern Master [the medium had made the same piece of equipment do double duty].

Anyway, the group decided to string the medium along to see more.

The guy, it developed, had a drinking problem [to put it

mildly] and the spirits who spoke through the trumpet at the next séance were slightly tipsy. As the séances continued the spirits got progressively drunker.

Before the final séance Bishop Pike and Ian Stevenson told the medium he must submit to a search. They found nothing suspicious on his person [Pike's slightly ribald comment was: "Well, he's all there!"].

It was also agreed that Diane Kennedy was to sit *inside* the cabinet with the medium.

This last séance was a madhouse. No spirits appeared while Diane was sitting in the cabinet [I'm not surprised] though the medium did manage to produce a small pinwheel of light, possibly by having coated a small piece of cloth with phosphorescent spray and then twirling it in the darkness.

After Diane Kennedy left the cabinet the real fun started. The trumpet spoke and the spirits were drunkenly belligerent. At one point Pike asked an august ecclesiastic [Bishop Somebody], who was speaking, to recite the Greek alphabet backwards—a cinch for such a great scholar— and the spirit politely told him to go to hell.

When Spraggett raised objections to something a spirit said, the trumpet, in the darkness, began beating him about the head, whereupon Pike tried to grab it and the trumpet flew through the air and landed at Marion Spraggett's feet. She, realizing the medium was manipulating it by an extension rod, promptly stepped on the trumpet bringing the séance to an abrupt conclusion.

Ian Stevenson frankly told the medium that in his medical judgment he was a terminal alcoholic and probably already had suffered brain damage. With true kindness he offered to give the medium psychiatric treatment if he would accept it.

The medium, a drunken, maudlin mess, refused to acknowledge his fakery but was forced to sign a statement that he would never attempt to exploit Bishop Pike's name in connection with his mediumship. He hastily scrawled his signature on the notarized form and crawled away.

The last Pike and the others saw of them, the medium and his cabinet attendant were staggering down the main street of Santa Barbara at one in the morning. She was carrying her shoes and the black curtain and he was wearing her potted-plant hat and her fur wrap and exclaiming at the top of his lungs: "Wendy, this reminds me of the time they ran us out of Moscow, Idaho!"

Pike's comment on the whole mad business was: "If anybody so much as mentions the word ectoplasm to me for a month I'll kill 'em!"

That poor sucker of a medium was different from scores of others only insofar as he bit off more than he could chew.

I never made that mistake. . . . But then I *was* smarter.

7/SEX IN THE SEANCE, or How to Lay a Ghost

The traditional term to "lay" a ghost—meaning to put it to rest—in the darkness of the séance room has taken on an altogether different meaning.

Earlier I mentioned astral necrophilia: making love to the dead. Well, it exists. A select clientele demands it. And some mediums provide it.

Of all the weird and sordid aspects of phony mediumship, this is the weirdest and most sordid. That's the way I felt as a medium and I still do. But clearly not all mediums agreed with me.

One medium named Naomi Carman Merkler, who looked like a truck driver in drag and claimed to be the granddaughter of Deborah, Queen of the Gypsies, boasted to me, "I'm a minister in the church . . . a lady in the parlor . . . a cook in the kitchen . . . a fraud in the séance room . . . and a whore in the bedroom. Of course, I'm a whore in the séance room too if the occasion arises!"

Mere gross hyperbole from a gross woman?

I thought so at the time. But I soon learned better.

There *are* sitters, real sickies, who actually believe—or delude themselves into thinking they believe—that a spirit can draw ectoplasm from the medium and produce the complete body [and I do mean complete] of a dead spouse or lover. The sitter has carnal intercourse with this spirit body which is as satisfyingly solid and responsive as the physical and goes on his or her way rejoicing in the reality of sex after death.

Too far out to believe? There was a time when I would have said so. Then one day, while filling in for a famous female medium, I gave a sitting to a middle-aged woman who was prosperously dressed but had a hungry look around the eyes and mouth.

We were sitting in darkness, of course, and I brought spirit greetings from the woman's dead husband through the trumpet, but she wasn't satisfied. There was something wrong, I knew, but what?

She began to tell her husband that she wanted the kind of sitting she got from the other medium, the woman for whom I was pinch-hitting.

My little girl spirit guide interrupted and said innocently, "Oops, your husband has lost the vibration, but we'll get him back in just a moment. Meanwhile we want to produce whatever you're used to. What is it you want your husband to do?"

The woman replied, "Well, I want him to make love to me in his materialized body like he does when the other medium is here!"

The trumpet clattered to the floor. I admit I dropped it from shock. That was the end of that séance.

Later, by digging, I found that the other medium kept a special phallic device, or *dildo,* by which she offered unique spirit consolation to that woman and several other sitters like her who were willing to pay special prices for the special services they demanded.

Some of the mediums I knew were virtually psychic prostitutes. In the séance room Brenda Himmel took on all comers. For a price. One whole family of second-generation mediums, male and female, were invited to leave Camp Chesterfield because their sexual escapades in the séance room were too open and notorious.

Sometimes, if the sitter was particularly attractive, the medium would be the one who initiated the séance sex. In these cases it was the medium's spirit guide, of course, who had astral relations with the sitter.

One male medium was a sort of verbal voyeur—he loved sexual conversation and pornography. In private sittings he used to masturbate while his spirit guide extracted from women sitters clinical information about their sexual experiences: how often, with whom, the anatomical details, postural procedures, number and mode of orgasms, and so on *ad nauseam.*

His excuse to the sitter for the erotic inquisition was, believe it or not, the necessity of such information in analyzing her body chemistry and balance for the fullest development of her psychic and spiritual gifts!

When excitable people, women especially, are psychologically sensitized by the powerful emotions—including the scarcely veiled eroticism—that pervade the séance room, anything can happen—and often does. At the risk of sounding too bizarre to be believed, let me tell you about one incident when, though a part of it, I was innocent of what actually happened.

A male medium was suffering sexual frustration, mainly because he never gave private sittings; it's during these, as a rule, that the medium does his seducing. His frustration became acute the day he and I were acting as co-mediums in a group séance of about thirty-five sitters, mostly women. Among them was a woman he had had his lustful eye on for quite some time. He decided to strike now or never.

The séance was in darkness, of course. Through the trumpet my spirit voices were droning on when the other medium quietly took his intended seducee by the hand and led her to a corner of the room. With whispered instructions to be quiet so as not to disturb the others, she was told that she was going to receive special spirit ministrations to "open your psychic center."

While the rest of us, including me, continued with our séance the woman had a thrilling spiritual experience all her own. Her psychic center opened very satisfactorily. The medium had sexual intercourse with her.

Later he told me about it with a coarse laugh. And the woman? She remained thrilled by what had happened and, we discovered, had rushed out to tell her equally pleased [well, almost] husband that the spirits had chosen her for a "wonderful" experience.

The woman mediums I knew evidently all had strong libidos. One, now over seventy, was certainly still going strong in her sixties. She had a boyfriend named Roy, much younger than she was, and the two of them used to take off on lost weekends. When they returned, Roy looked exhausted.

The male mediums—well, often they were sexually ambiguous. I think that's the fairest way to put it: ambiguous.

I once gave a private sitting to a prominent Indianapolis doctor who in greeting me said, "Well, I've met many of the queens of spiritualism, but it's refreshing to meet someone masculine enough to be called the prince!"

Sex, of course, has traditionally pervaded the occult just as it has religion. There is a close affinity between the mystical impulse and the sex drive, and maybe it's not surprising that people, and not only mediums, sometimes get the two confused.

Now that we've all been vaguely Freudianized, there's hardly anyone so unsophisticated as to deny the patent erotic element in many mystical experiences. St. Teresa with her vision of the angel thrusting into her a flaming spear, at which she swooned with divine love, was obviously experiencing misplaced sex. At least, that's my view.

Everyone knows that traditionally the rites of voodoo and black magic are associated with sexual debauch. And more than one psychical researcher has commented on the high erotic content in mediumship.

Observers said that Eusapia Palladino used to experience obvious orgasmic reactions during her séances and had a marked propensity for handsome male sitters. One psychical researcher called her "frighteningly erotic."

Sex certainly invaded the séance room with the famous and beautiful Margery the Medium. There were persistent rumors that she won some supporters by using more than her psychic powers. One researcher, Paul Tabori, reports as fact that Hereward Carrington, a noted investigator who brought in a favorable verdict on Margery's mediumship, had a sexual affair with her.

Margery, a comely lady by all accounts, conducted many of her sittings in the nude [after first being thoroughly examined by a committee of doctors, an ordeal from which apparently she was never known to shrink]. The medium's state of undress was supposed to rule out fraud. Since during the production of the phenomena Margery became quite active and often threw her feet into the lap of one sitter while her head was lolling in the lap of another [all in the dark, of course], at times the proceedings must have taken on the characteristics of what today would be called a "group grope."

Also, numerous accounts testify that Margery's ectoplasm showed a marked propensity for coming from her vagina and returning thereto.

The late Nandor Fodor told Allen Spraggett in personal conversation his impressions of Margery in her last phase, after the death of her husband, when she was descending deeper and deeper into alcoholism. Fodor said that when he stayed in the Crandon home with other investigators, the medium often knocked on his door at night. Dr. Fodor said he felt pity for her—a once-beautiful woman who was like a faded and forgotten picture.

There was a notorious sex-and-spiritualism case back in the thirties involving a New York medium who ran a sort of spirit massage parlor. Officially, the medium's clients, most of whom were middle-aged women, visited his ten-room apartment on Riverside Drive to receive healing treatments from a spirit doctor. This doctor, a Frenchman who had been dead for seventy or eighty years, would materialize, ask the woman to undress and lie on the bed, then perform his healing ministrations which consisted of running his hands over the patient's entire body.

Many clients apparently found the treatments very effective in relieving headaches, backaches, and all sorts of other things. For some, however, the experience evidently wasn't what they had expected, and they complained to the authorities.

The upshot was that a policewoman in civilian dress presented herself for a spirit massage. As the robed figure was attending to her infirmities, she suddenly reached out and snapped on a pair of handcuffs. The spirit turned into the medium, whose name was Emerson Gilbert. The next stop was court, where a Magistrate Goldstein handed out a fine and a stern lecture.

The February 10, 1973, issue of *Psychic News*, Britain's spiritualist weekly, gave an account of the bizarre sexual mediumship of a London man accused of invoking spirits, the Virgin Mary, and even Christ to lure women into bed with him.

This medium told a woman sitter that she had been "chosen by God to have a spirit child" by him. Later, when he was exposed, the medium pleaded that he wasn't to blame—the spirits were.

"When the entities enter my body," he said, "they do dreadful things. Sometimes they make me try to kill myself. Sometimes they want me to have sex.

"I'm in a trance all the time but I never really do anything like that because my own spirit guides always intervene before anything really improper happens. They pull me out of it."

The woman who went to the medium because she was "troubled by spirits" was told by him that a spirit had entered her womb.

"One day," said the woman, "he told me he had a message from his spirit guides. 'It is willed by God and the spirit world and Jesus Christ that you shall have a child by spirit,' he told me.

"The medium told me I was to have intercourse by transfiguration. I would appear to be having sex with him but really it would be with a spirit.

"He told me the child was going to be a boy. He would be one of the greatest psychics ever known. He said the world would know of this child."

For some time, said the woman, she was completely under the medium's influence. Often when she was with him she experienced something like a trance. She remembered few details of her times with him and what really happened.

The woman's sister, in a sworn statement, described an incident in which the medium committed an "outrage" on the woman and then turned into a gorilla!

The sister recalled that one night, when the medium was at the woman's home, the two of them went upstairs. When they didn't return, the sister investigated and found them in bed.

"I rushed over," said the sister, "and pulled him off her. I was very angry. I shouted at him to get out.

"Then the medium started acting like a gorilla. He was

breathing heavily, snuffling and waving his arms about. His face was twisted. It was like a horror film."

Two women reporters, checking out the allegations about the medium, used themselves as decoys. They visited him, complaining of being harassed by evil spirits, and were told that the only way to exorcise such spirits was by having sexual intercourse with the medium.

"He made sexual advances," one of the women reporters said, "and kept trying to persuade me to have intercourse."

"This is a very terrible condition you have," the medium told her. "I have to make love to you with this entity. . . . That would clear the condition completely."

Then the medium's spirit guides came through, one of whom spoke with what was described as a "comic" accent.

"God bless you," said the guide, "I, Atonga, talk with you through my medi [sic]. Let the entity take its course. You will then feel much better. You will feel in harmony and in peace with spirit.

"It means that my medi must link with you. In de linking the condition will be completely cleared. You will be better, one hundred per cent. And if you have child, it will be boy."

This case, reported by the spiritualists' own press, dramatizes how kooky and kinky sex mediumship can become.

One woman sitter of mine was, so far as I was concerned, a terminal case of astral necrophilia. She came from Chicago, was married, had a nice husband and a young son, but was hung up on a spirit lover named Stanley.

At Camp Chesterfield, where I met her, she came to me as often as I would allow. [She would have come two or three times a day if I had accepted her bookings.] She seemed fairly rational in the sittings until she started talking to this Stanley character, oohing and aahing about his prowess as a lover [he was dead, remember] and the wonderful astral children they had!

This woman actually believed that Stanley came to her astrally every night and made love to her and that she had conceived and borne these spirit children.

At first I tried to reason her out of the fantasy. She listened to what I said and seemed to accept it, but she returned next time as crazy as ever over Stanley. Finally I refused to give her any more sittings.

In his book. *The Haunted Mind,* Nandor Fodor discusses sex and mediumship. He describes how one male medium, Willie Schneider, whose spirit guide was Mina, a girl, used to embrace male sitters during his trances. He quotes one woman medium who told him that when she went into trance it was as though "a hand were massaging my womb."

A bizarre incident Fodor mentions concerned Madame D'Esperance, the famous medium, whose materialized spirit guide Yolande was raped in the dark by a sitter. The medium, says Fodor, spent two years recovering from the experience.

Interestingly, Fodor reports a case in London in 1922 which parallels the sex-in-the-séance-room I've described. It seems that a woman named Gertrude had a dead lover, Charles, for whom she yearned ardently. Gertrude shopped around from medium to medium until she found one who brought through her beloved Charles. He proved to be as warm in his affections as he had been when on earth.

Each séance ended with the medium, on coming out of her trance, finding herself in Gertrude's arms. Since the medium was also a woman, this was somewhat awkward and unsatisfactory. But Charles found a way.

The medium was prompted [by Charles, of course] to

acquire an instrument such as I've previously described, by which she was able with perfect satisfaction to fulfill the spirit's desire for full physical union with his beloved Gertrude.

As Fodor tells it, everything was bliss for three years, until one day Gertrude's husband, who was impotent or something, found the instrument and stepped on it, smashing it beyond repair. The woman's astral assignations with her dead lover ceased.

Taken with the account of my own experience, Fodor's story raises the question of just how common such sexual séances really are. More common, perhaps, than even I suspect.

To me, of course, sex in the séance room is merely a logical, though particularly nasty, extension of the basic premise of fraudulent mediumship: give the customer what he [or she] wants. What it *is* doesn't matter; what it *pays* does.

Another reaction, of course, is pity for those who are so lonely and alienated from normal human companionship that they have to cohabit with a ghost. Here, as in other areas of life, the services of the phony medium do not help the sitter—they hinder him or her in developing the inner resources to face life realistically.

As long as a person is dependent on a medium, he'll never find the strength to become independent. And without that, life is hardly worth living. . . .

8/THE UNMAKING OF A MEDIUM: How It All Ended

With all the money flowing in—with the glamour, excitement, and adulation of being a successful medium—was I happy?

No.

For one thing, I was always aware, like all mediums, that most people looked down on us, that we weren't really respectable.

Oh, we had important friends to whom we were more than respectable, but society as a whole disdained us. And nobody enjoys being a freak, an oddity, a suspected fraud, a shady character, no matter how much glamour goes with it.

Then there was the little matter of conscience. Most mediums probably are what psychiatrists call sociopathic. They have a moral block, a defective conscience. Things that other people consider wrong, they consider legitimate. Cheating, lying, stealing, conning—these are sanctified in the ethics of mediumship as I knew it.

Though most mediums apparently manage to anesthetize their consciences [if they have any], I couldn't. Not completely. Looking in the mirror, I'd feel a pang of something I recognized as shame (it had been so long since I'd acknowledged the feeling that it was unfamiliar).

Sometimes in my cups I'd think, "What sort of creep am I? Could anybody without a sick mind be proud of what I'm doing?"

It was such spasms of conscience that made me start giving charity sittings for people who couldn't afford our regular fees. This gesture was a feeble attempt to fan whatever spark of normal, decent human feeling was left in me. I had to do *something* that wasn't motivated entirely by self gain.

The conscience spasms were interspersed with periods of relative enthusiasm for what I was doing—even, at times, a manic euphoria [usually induced by a particularly successful séance but increasingly fortified in my case by alcohol and in the case of many mediums by drugs].

There were longer spells of gray flatness when I felt neither guilt nor gladness but simply went through the motions of living, finding my mediumship an escape from troubling thoughts: a routine that had become comfortable, safe, and—simply because it was so familiar—reassuring.

Then something fresh would prick my conscience, and the cycle—self-recrimination, enthusiasm, flatness—would start all over. On and on I went, round and round, caught on the Devil's carousel. . . .

What led me to renounce the lie I was living, to try to build a truthful life, was chiefly the example of a remarkable woman—remarkable for her simple human goodness—who became my adoptive mother: Florence Hutchison. This chapter in my life is in some ways more amazing than anything I've recounted, but unlike the other parts, it is a story of truth, not deceit.

This chapter started a few years ago at Camp Chesterfield. A woman whom I had never seen before sought me out for a sitting. She'd come all the way from Bartlesville, Oklahoma, she said, because of what others had told her about my psychic powers. I must help her!

My first inclination was to tell her to get lost. But Florence Hutchison is a hard person to say that to. If she had been one of the typical bitchy ghostmongers, I would have brushed her off in a moment, but she really was a kindly and appealing lady. So I simply told her I was sorry, I was booked for two weeks ahead, but if she came back then I might be able to see her.

Well, she was with a friend who had sat with me and, as it happened, had another appointment for the next day. She offered Florence her appointment, and I agreed to that.

Going to the files under the Cathedral for the usual pre-séance research, I found myself stymied. Florence Hutchison had never been to Chesterfield before and there was nothing on her in the files. However, since she looked like such an agreeable sort, I decided to take her "cold," as we mediums said, and "pluck the feathers off her" [a term for picking information from a sitter without letting her realize she is telling it to you].

The next day at the séance she did prove most cooperative, and soon things were rolling merrily along. I presented her with her spirit guide, whom she had never met before, and she seemed suitably impressed. And when I brought through her mother and father in spirit, she accepted them gladly.

Then she asked a question which I'll never forget. It changed my life.

"Can you help me find an important legal document I've lost?" Florence inquired.

Her deceased husband would know where it was, she said. Could you speak to him about it?

The document in question was a will, but she didn't reveal that at the time. I was on the spot! There was no way of ducking the question except by pretending to "lose trance" and to suddenly wake up, claiming that something had interrupted the spirit communication. But that seemed so obvious I disdained using it.

"Well, how the hell do I get out of this?" I asked myself.

Then I said the first thing that came into my head, which was: "You have a metal file cabinet at home, the portable one, and it has a false top in it. There is a key to the false top in the bottom under some papers. The document is in that false top."

It was a stupid-sounding thing, but what the hell, I thought, the woman wasn't likely to return to Chesterfield, and it got her out of my hair at that moment. That was all I really cared about.

The answer seemed to satisfy Florence. She fairly flew out of the séance room and, I learned later, rushed home to Oklahoma that very day.

My mother [as she later became] has set down her own account of that experience and its astonishing sequel:

"My husband, Alphonso Deville Hutchison, whom I called A.D., was an independent oil producer. He was killed in an accident on February 19, 1962. There was no trace of a will, though he had made one. A trace of the original, I mean. My husband's attorney had a copy of the will, but this wasn't legal because it hadn't been duly witnessed. Anyway, we needed the original. But where was it?

"Almost a year went by and the attorneys were getting ready to file a lost will in probate court. I still held out hope that the original would turn up. I knew A.D. kept it around the house somewhere. But I'd gone through the tin box where he kept his papers and the will wasn't in there. Nor anywhere else that I looked.

"Then a spiritualist couple told me about Camp Chesterfield and said that I should visit it and get a sitting with Lamar. He's the world's best medium, they said; if he can't help you, nobody can. I flew to Indiana the next day.

"In the séance, believing I was talking with my husband, I asked, 'Did so-and-so take the document?' mentioning a certain cousin of whom I was suspicious. The spirit voice said, 'Oh no.'

"So I said, 'Well darling, where is it? I've looked everywhere that I thought you could put a paper.'

"He said, 'Well, you know that I've got a tin box. . . .' I said, 'I've looked in that tin box.'

"'But there's a false top to that box,' he said, 'and the key to it is in the box under some papers. Look in that false top and you'll find the document.'

"So I rushed home to Oklahoma, arriving about two o'clock in the morning, and boy I went downstairs as fast as I could go and I took that tin box and turned it upside down and shook it until the key fell out. Then I looked under the lid and, lo and behold, there was the false top all right! I opened it with the key—and found the will."

After this experience my mother was convinced that I was the greatest medium alive. Nothing could have persuaded her I wasn't genuine. In fact, much later I myself had a job convincing her of that!

How did I come up with the false top on the tin box?

Well, it was an unusual occurrence, but I simply attribute it to the fact that I had given thousands of readings and by the law of averages had to make a few lucky guesses. This one was incredibly lucky, I'll admit, but not enough to make me believe that I was a true medium.

However, that wasn't the last unusual experience involving the woman who was to become my adoptive mother. Because of her attachment to my mediumship and to me, she moved to Florida and became a regular attender at the church. Once, during an apport séance, the spirits delivered to her an old-fashioned lavalier. It was part of a bunch of junk that I'd bought for apports. Why I selected that particular item for my mother I have no idea.

However, from my mother's point of view that lavalier turned out to have quite a history. Here is how she tells the story:

"When the apport tumbled into my hands out of the trumpet, I knew it was a brooch of some kind because I could feel the pin and the chain on it. But in the pitch-darkness I couldn't see exactly what it was.

"When the lights came on I examined it, found it was a lavalier, and said to myself, 'Why, do you know, that looks like the very one my brother gave me when I was just turning sixteen.' I later had lost my brother's gift at school in the little town of Delaware, Oklahoma.

"The more I looked at the lavalier, the more certain I was that it was the same one. After fifty years! Was it possible?

"So I thought, 'Well, there's one person who'll be able to identify it: my brother. I'll see what he says.'

"I just took the lavalier in to him and said, 'Buck, I want you to look at this. It was given to me. Have you ever seen it before?'

"My brother looked at it and said, 'Why, that's the lavalier I gave you when you were sixteen and you lost it. Where in the world did you get it?'

" 'Oh, it was given to me,' I said. And he said, 'Well, I'm glad you got it back even if you did have to wait fifty years.' "

This story of my mother's is one that I cannot explain.

Florence saw in me, she said, an uncanny likeness to her son, Charles, who was killed in the service in World War Two, and as we grew closer she eventually decided that she wanted to adopt me legally as her son. The deep affection

I felt for her led me, in spite of obvious reasons for hesitating, to agree, and I became her son.

Yet even after the adoption, and with all the sincere love I had for her, I continued to dupe my mother along with the others in the séance room. How could I do otherwise without removing my mask to her? And I was afraid that what she saw then might appear so ugly she would shrink from me in horror.

My growing closeness to my mother and the honesty and integrity she represented was the biggest single factor in my decision to give up mediumship. But another was my becoming a Mason.

I joined the Masonic fraternity while I was a medium, recommended in all good faith by a member of my church. In spite of myself I began taking the Masonic obligations to heart; they became rather sacred to me. I know this may sound incredible, since I was then a professional desecrator of things most people consider holy, but nevertheless it's true. The spirit of Masonry worked in me like a leaven.

Every day the contradiction between the lie I lived, and the kind of truth my mother embodied, became uglier to me. Séances were approached with increasing revulsion; they were no longer fun and games, but rather a ghastly parody of which I was sick to death.

Beside the mediums with whom I worked, my mother was, quite simply, a saint in hell. For once in my life I had met a real person, and I wanted some of her integrity for myself. I wanted to give whatever good was left in me a chance to grow—otherwise there seemed no point in going on.

Looking ahead, if I stayed in mediumship I saw only deepening gloom. All the mediums I've known or known about have had tragic endings.

The Fox sisters, who started it all, wound up as alcoholic derelicts. William Slade, famed for his slate-writing tricks, died insane in a Michigan sanitarium. Margery the Medium lay on her deathbed a hopeless drunk. The celebrated Arthur Ford fought the battle of the bottle to the very end and lost. And the inimitable Mable Riffle, boss of Camp Chesterfield—well, when she died it was winter and freezing cold, and her body had to be held until a thaw for burial; the service was in the Cathedral at Chesterfield. Very few attended.

Wherever I looked it was the same: mediums, at the end of a tawdry life, dying a tawdry death.

The change going on within me led to increasing friction with Raoul. Finally we had a confrontation in which I told him I was sick and tired of the whole business—the fraud bit, the drug bit, the drinking bit, the entire thing—that I wanted to make the church into a legitimate Christian metaphysical congregation teaching the power of prayer and positive thinking and cut out the séance-room charades.

Raoul simply said no, it wouldn't pay well enough. So I said, "Well, if that's the way you feel, there's going to have to be a showdown."

And there was.

That showdown and its sequel may be the most incredible thing of my whole mediumistic career. And the most revealing.

Shortly after our confrontation Raoul, during a development class meeting at the church attended by about a hundred people, suddenly seemed to lose control. His rage and resentment against me just broke loose, and in front of the class, he threw a temper tantrum. Screaming that he wasn't going to be undermined any longer, he demanded that the board members present gather immediately in another part of the church for a closed meeting.

As Raoul raged, I realized that this wasn't as impromptu as it seemed—that no doubt he had gone to all the board members in advance and poisoned them against me. His tactic, it turned out, was to head off any charges of mine by accusing me first of being fraudulent in my mediumship!

The meeting was convened, and all the members of the board were there. Raoul began by saying that the dissension and confusion which I had been sowing in the church had to stop.

"I've already told these board members that your billet-reading is fraudulent," he said, pointing to everybody but two women.

I said, "Oh well, that's true. It is fraudulent. But let's have the whole truth. Let's tell these board members you've primed that so is my trumpet mediumship fraudulent, my materializations, my apports, my card writing, my precipitation on silk, my spirit photographs, my clairvoyance—the works! It's all fraudulent!"

(Why had Raoul singled out only my billet-reading? Probably because at a previous church meeting I had refused ever again to do billet-reading, and in order to explain this embarrassing cessation of a popular phenomenon, Raoul told the board members he had discovered that that phase of my mediumship was fake and demanded that I drop it.)

"But let's not just tell them about me," I said to Raoul, "let's tell them about you. That every phase of mediumship that you demonstrate is fraudulent. And that every phase that every medium in the world demonstrates is fraudulent!"

Then I stopped and stared at him in silence.

In a quiet voice, Raoul said, "It's true."

And I said, "All right, it's up to you people. Unless this church can become a legitimate Christian organization, I'll walk out that door and never return."

One woman spoke up and said, "Well, I agree with you. If it isn't right, my spirit people have taught me through you that I shouldn't be any part of it."

(This incredible statement—incredible in the light of what I had just revealed about the "spirit people"—threw me for a loop. I thought, are they all quite mad?)

Another woman got up and said that she agreed; things had to change or else.

These two women were the only ones to express support for me. Some of the board members seemed bewildered by the confusing turn of events. Others, in spite of the revelations, were outspokenly behind Raoul. This, in fact, represented the final mood of the meeting. The board expressed confidence in Raoul and voted to leave matters entirely in his hands.

"Whatever Raoul decides," said one woman, "is what we want to do."

"In spite of what you've heard?" I interjected. "In spite of what he himself has admitted to you here?"

With that one board member, a very polished lady in her seventies who thought she was fifty-five, stood up, fixed me with a withering look, and snapped, "Sit down and shut up!"

(Interestingly, this woman's husband, who all along opposed her obsession with the spirits, has since died, leaving her wealthy, and I understand that she pours money into Raoul's new church—in spite of what she knows about spiritualism's inner workings. Who can fathom such a mind?)

"Not here I won't" was my reply. I got up and took my mother's arm, and we left the church. One board member, a woman, followed. The rest stayed, staring sullenly after us.

I was crushed. I knew how easy it was to make people believe a lie, but I didn't expect that the same people, confronted with the lie, would choose it over the truth.

One of the board members, George Mathern, who had

moved from Ohio to join the church and had given generously of both cash and property, had said to Raoul, "Do you mean to say that you duped me?" and got the reply, "That's right, George." Yet even after that, he stayed in his seat beside Raoul and is still active in spiritualism to this day.

The true-believer syndrome merits study by science. What is it that compels a person, past all reason, to believe the unbelievable? How can an otherwise sane individual become so enamored of a fantasy, an imposture, that even after it's exposed in the bright light of day he still clings to it—indeed, clings to it all the harder?

The true-believer syndrome is the greatest thing phony mediums have going for them. No amount of logic can shatter a faith consciously based on a lie.

I think Raoul had those people on the church board virtually hypnotized. Every one of them, with a single exception, had had numerous private sittings with him, and he did have exceptional skill in brainwashing people. He had turned them into unthinking zombies.

In our library was a copy of Hitler's *Mein Kampf,* which Raoul read avidly. He adopted in his mediumship some of the specific techniques in mass psychology that Hitler described. Looking through that book and noting the many passages Raoul marked, and his comments, was very revealing.

My mother, of course, wasn't under Raoul's spell, and the board meeting and its revelations hit her like an earthquake. By the time we got home, she was virtually in a state of shock.

It was then I said to her, "Mother, I'm going to tell you the truth about everything. And if, when I'm through, you don't want me to be your son any longer, I'll understand. You just tell me, and I'll walk out the door with only the suit I'm wearing and never come back."

And I meant every word, as she knew.

So I told her the whole sordid story—how Raoul and I started out in mediumship; the files on sitters; the phony apports, materializations, and trumpet séances; the cynical financial exploitation of people—all of it. I spared her no sordid detail. It rushed out of me in a murky wave, a catharsis, a release. I felt like a penitent making confession to save his soul.

And my mother's reaction?

This is how she described it: "After Lamar finished his story I didn't speak for a few minutes. I couldn't speak. When I found my voice my first words, as I recall, were, 'I can't believe it!'

" 'Well, you'd better,' said Lamar, 'because it's true. And now what do you want me to do?'

"I said, 'Well, I think I would be a very poor mother if in your trouble I were to forsake you. No my son, you *are* my son. I'll share it with you.' "

Later I returned to the church for one last time. I raided the steel vault where all the séance paraphernalia were stored: ectoplasm, apports, and the rest. Backing my car to the door of the church, I dumped as much of the chiffon and other junk as I could into the trunk, then roared off, no doubt streaming ectoplasm.

The next time Raoul went to the vault to fish out his spirit garb—for him it was business as usual—he found it as bare as Mother Hubbard's cupboard.

To make my renunciation of mediumship complete, I knew there were other things I yet had to do. Seeking out a Masonic friend, I poured forth to him the whole story. At my request he went with me to the authorities. I turned myself in to the Internal Revenue Service for evasion of income tax. (I eventually paid all back taxes in full.) I also visited the FBI, the county sheriff's office, and the state attorney-general. To all these I made full confession of my years of fraud.

No police investigation of any medium was launched as a result of my action nor, to my knowledge, did the Internal Revenue Service look into the matter of mediumistic bookkeeping. One reason for official reluctance to do anything may be an exaggerated concept of religious liberty. Apparently the last thing a public official in this country wants is for some sect like the spiritualists to scream bloody murder about religious persecution. At any rate, whatever the reason, the mediums continue unmolested.

As a matter of fact, my former partner is doing better than ever. He got a new apprentice to train in mediumship and continued the church. As a bribe to all those who stayed with him, he ordained them; from twelve-year-old children to eighty-year-old women: all received ordination certificates as spiritualist ministers.

A recent newspaper advertisement by Raoul's church is typical. It proclaims:

"South's largest psychic-metaphysical congregation. . . . The fantastically different church where worship is a pleasure. . . . Where outstanding psychic phenomena is [sic] a common occurrence. . . . A modern day school of the prophets. . . . All nine gifts of the Spirit are in evidence. . . . Demonstrated in a setting of classical art and beauty. . . . The last word in up-to-date New Age Philosophy and Psychic Phenomena. . . . A center of Divine revelation, prophetic utterances and Spirit communications. . . . An organization destined to success even in the face of fierce opposition."

Yes, the ghost business is booming. . . .

9/THE PSYCHIC MAFIA

One summer's day when I was serving as a staff medium at Camp Chesterfield—"Hub of World Spiritualism"—an incident occurred which for me symbolizes the utter cynicism of the psychic mafia.

A medium's wife was working in the Sun Flower Hotel on the camp grounds (rooms: four dollars a night) and received an emergency phone call for one of the guests. The call was from a sheriff's department. The guest, a woman, was unavailable to take the call, since she was at a public séance in the Cathedral.

"Well," said the policeman at the other end of the line, "we would like to leave a message that Mrs. So-and-so contact us as soon as possible on an urgent family matter."

"Why, whatever's happened?" asked the medium's wife.

"Well," the policeman hesitated, "you see, her son was killed in a car accident."

The medium's wife hurried to the Cathedral, where Willard Warren was just about to go out on the platform to give spirit messages. And the rest you can anticipate. . . .

Yes, that's right—the woman heard the tragic news from

Willard Warren in the guise of a communication from her spirit loved ones that her son had "crossed over" just a few minutes earlier, after being killed in a car accident.

The woman went into hysterics, and everybody else who heard the message gasped at this marvelous proof of spirit communication!

The mentality that is capable of such heartless manipulation of people's most wounded feelings is in my judgment capable of even more.

I am not being melodramatic but factual when I report that since renouncing mediumship I have received threatening phone calls. "Lay off the mediums or else," muffled voices warned.

In my days as a medium I had sat in on meetings at which were discussed various means of expediting the demise of certain elderly folk who were sure to leave a lot of money to the spiritualist cause. One woman medium claimed to be an expert in poisons that were virtually untraceable. To my knowledge no actual fatal foul play resulted from these discussions but believe me they were held in a spirit of deadly seriousness not fun.

I was so sure that the mediums would try to liquidate me because I knew too much and might spill it that I bought a black suit to be buried in. (Funny, even thinking about dying, proper dress was important to me.)

One night, a few months after I had made the break with the psychic mafia, I was strolling across the lawn of our Tampa home when a shot rang out. Instinctively I hurled myself to the ground and lay still, feeling my heart racing. When I finally got up and hurried into the house my knees were like jelly and I went into the bathroom and threw up.

A car backfire? No, it was definitely a shot. I confirmed that the next day when I dug a rifle slug out of the wall of the house. Whether the marksman's intention had been to kill me or to scare me I can't say, but I was scared all right!

After this incident I moved my mother and myself out of that house. We sold it at a sacrifice and took an apartment for greater security.

Before moving, while we were still in the big house, I bought a pistol and took to sleeping with it under my pillow. One morning I forgot to put it inside the nightstand as I usually did, and when our maid, Annie Laurie, made the bed, she saw the wicked-looking thing peeking out from under the pillow. Screams!

My mother, knowing I liked practical jokes, rushed in, thinking I had left a rubber spider or something where the maid would find it, but she realized very quickly that the gun was no toy. She briskly took it and locked it in a cupboard.

The three years immediately after I left mediumship were my real dark night of the soul. I went into virtual seclusion. With my mediumship, I also had given up all my former friends. Anyway, I was in no mood to meet or see anybody. The festering sore of fraud in me, which I had purged, had been replaced by a profound emptiness. I was disoriented, rootless, rudderless, drifting, looking desperately for an anchor.

Anything to do with the occult was repugnant to me. I took my more than two thousand books on mediumship, psychical research, and related topics and consigned them to the incinerator. Any mention of séances or psychics in the newspapers or on television nauseated me. I was sick to death of the whole business!

The rebuilding of my self-esteem and a sane perspective on life didn't come easily. I was like someone who, having spent thirteen years living in a crazy house looking at ev-

erything in distorting mirrors, now had to get used to seeing things normally. My eyes refused to adjust. My image
of myself, of other people, of the world was distorted; I
couldn't help it.

My mother's unfailing love and support proved my
mainstay in that perilous emotional time. She always understood, never judged. Without her I would never have
made it.

And there were other people who heartened me and
helped me to see life whole again. One was my Masonic
brother, William Twiss, whose wise counsel and fatherly
kindness was always there when I needed it. There were
others who helped me by their example, such as one woman from whom I had taken several thousand dollars as a
medium and whom I felt I owed a personal apology. She
listened to my story gravely, then said, "Well Lamar, if the
good Lord forgives, how can I stand in your way? I forgive
you too."

It was even hard to totally dissociate myself from my
past. Occasionally I'd run into former sitters who, knowing
only that I had given up my mediumship, would ask, "Are
you doing readings again?" Many spiritualists assumed
that I had lost my powers, presumably because of unwor-
thiness. No doubt this was the party line promulgated by
my former associates.

Did I ever tell my story to the newspapers?

No. I thought about it but rejected the idea.

"What's the point?" I said to someone who had urged
me to blow the whole thing wide open in the press. "Sure, I
could make things hot for the church here. But it would be
merely a local scandal, forgotten in a few days. It would
have no lasting effect. No, if I ever tell my story it will be to
do some real good."

When I contemplated putting this story down on paper,
it wasn't in a spirit of vindictiveness. I want nobody's scalp.

But I did feel with increasing urgency that my story should be told as a warning of those so-called spiritual shepherds who have become sheep-shearers, thieves, and robbers— wolves in sheep's clothing.

Who can measure the human misery that spiritualism and its false claims and broken hopes leaves in its murky wake?

I know of one elderly woman who gave thousands to our church, now shut away friendless and penniless in a nursing home. Another woman—and how many more like her?—suffered a stroke induced at least in part, I'm sure, by the conflicts and upheavals caused by preying mediums.

I know scores of people, professionals such as doctors and teachers, who were so enamored of the fantasies of spiritualism that they tore up roots and relocated half-way across the country to be near a favorite medium. (Many did this because of me.) The personal and family dislocations, the emotional pain, the career setbacks and financial losses, are incalculable.

Those who are sucked into the dark whirlpool of the psychic mafia often pay too high a price. . . .

The web of evil in which I was once enmeshed should be exposed. This was my growing conviction. But how and when?

Well, one day I was contacted by Canon William Rauscher of Woodbury, New Jersey. He had heard of me and my experiences from my Masonic brother, Bill Twiss. Canon Rauscher said he too was a Mason. He wanted to hear my personal history from me, so I told it to him.

"This is an enormously important story," he said later, "and one which must be told. You can do a great service to the cause of truth and psychical research."

Rauscher invited Allen Spraggett to cooperate in the

project as a professional writer and psychic investigator. Spraggett agreed with Rauscher's assessment: my story was important; it must be told.

And so this book came into being. . . .

In 1974, Bill Rauscher arranged for me to speak to the annual conference of Spiritual Frontiers Fellowship in Chicago—as "Mr. X" because we didn't want to blow my cover before this book was published—about my life as a phony medium. That lecture was an ordeal for me. As I stood on the platform looking out over an audience of some two thousand, I saw familiar faces which didn't belong to SFF. They were members of my old fraternity, there to spy, no doubt. One of them, a medium whom I had known well, sat slumped in his seat with his head down while I spoke. Not once did he look up to meet my gaze.

The lecture was brief, low-key. I simply hit the high spots of my fraudulent career, warning that audience of mainly sincere seekers of the pitfalls and booby traps strewn along the path to truth by those who prefer to keep men believing profitable lies.

After the lecture I did a vanishing act. The last thing I wanted was to see anyone, talk to anyone, answer anyone's questions. Frankly, I felt that as an individual I wasn't important; it was my story that mattered. *That's* what they should be concerned with. And that feeling is stronger today than ever.

However, I'm no longer a recluse. There is a place, I believe, for my talking about what happened to me. As one comment on my Chicago lecture which reached me later put it, "His former darkness can be our light."

Like an albatross, I carry my past around my neck. This came back with renewed force when I returned from Chicago and found that my lecture had triggered fresh threats and warnings to "lay off." In my lecture I had mentioned that this book was being written and the threats intimated that if the book were published the results might be fatal for me.

Exaggerating? No, I'm not. These renewed threats and warnings to suppress this book alarmed my mother and me enough that we moved again. Even now, my precise whereabouts are known to only a few trusted individuals. The psychic mafia plays rough.

To show how active the psychic mafia is currently—right now, as I write these words—I made it a point to get hold of a secret list of likely sitters now circulating among mediums in the Miami area.

This list, which runs to more than 400 names, includes such exquisite details as these:

"Do not give this man anything he writes on a billet. Do not bring any spirit he asks for. He is constantly testing, though a believer. His mother and father were Russian and were Jewish. Don't tell him she's with Jesus, etc. . . . In view of all, this is a good guy. . . .

"This man received personal letter from Nehru, prime minister of India about gift of two elephants to Miami Zoo. He is a Rev. and has a group called the Round Table. . . .

"She is a psychiatric nurse. . . . One psychiatrist once told her she should sell real estate because she could talk his patients into taking elect. shock treatments. Called the doctor, Dr. Andy."

There really is little I can add to the story I've told; it speaks for itself. How could anything be more eloquent? The lessons are there for even the blind to see.

But will those with eyes see the truth? I wonder again after reading about a movie called THE FILMING OF A GHOST (*Psychic News*, Nov. 30, 1974).

This forty-minute motion picture, which has been shown to psychic groups around the country and in November, 1974, was telecast by CITY-TV in Toronto, shows streams of ectoplasm and a spirit materialization produced by Camp Silver Belle medium Warren Smith. (The film crew used infrared equipment in the pitch-black séance room.)

The producer of the film and its narrator, Darrell Random, a spiritualist, calls Smith "one of the truly great psychics in the world today."

The narration makes it plain that several times during the séance the medium insisted that the film crew stop their cameras for fear of injuring in some way the delicate ectoplasm. These no doubt were precisely the times when it would have been most interesting to keep the cameras running.

The materialized figure in the film looks just like the ones I produced. The streams of ectoplasm could have come from my old trunk. The methods of mediumship depicted in *The Filming of a Ghost* are quite familiar to me and should be to you after reading this book.

What about my present philosophy and outlook on life?

Well, I'm still long on questions and relatively short on answers, but I can offer a sort of personal minicredo.

I believe in God. I believe that God is the sustaining power of the universe and that everything expresses this power. Even evil, I believe, is potential good—a learning experience. Through my own experiences, disgusting as they are to me, I see that I have become a better person. Certainly I've learned lessons which I doubt could have come any other way.

In spite of all that's happened to me and the unsavory characters I've known, I still believe that basically everyone is good. A cliché, but I believe it.

I don't hate people for their wrongdoing, even the phony mediums. In fact, I have great sympathy for them, for I remember that once I was one of them.

I believe, as one woman remarked, "If they really knew

better they'd *do* better." If a person really knows better, he *will* do better. All evil is in some sense ignorance—of what man really is and what he was made for and the kind of life he can live.

I'm told that Socrates said something like this: "To know the good is to do it."

Life after death?

I believe in it. I believe that human beings maintain their individuality after death. I believe that we go on to higher and better expressions of ourselves than those which we are now expressing. I believe that evolution, growth, is the whole thing: mankind evolves, it doesn't regress. I believe that, in spite of all I've seen and experienced.

Extrasensory perception and psychic phenomena?

I believe that the individual can have his or her own private psychic experiences—that there is such a thing as ESP. But when it comes to paying a medium to do it for you—beware!

Communication with the dead is something I would urge you to avoid—I mean even the idea of it, the possibility of it. At least through a professional medium. Trying to communicate with the dead has been the downfall of many individuals, as my story amply and tragically reveals.

There is so much in the real world to enchant you, thrill you, elevate you. Why immure yourself in the darkness of the medium's cabinet where spirits "peep and mutter" and human folly falls prey to human greed?

I believe in life not death. I believe in light not darkness. I believe in the strength that comes from standing on one's own two feet rather than hobbling on the crutches of a deluded faith in a fraudulent medium.

Find your own way in the uncertainties of life. With God's help you can do it.

BIBLIOGRAPHY

The authors believe this bibliography to be the most comprehensive of its kind in a book such as this for the general reader. It includes, besides objective and critical works on spiritualism, many hard-to-find titles on such associated subjects as stage mentalism, carnival torture feats, and the specific methods of fraud used by particular mediums: for example, the "regurgitation" mediumship of Helen Duncan.

Readers who wish to go deeply into the psychology and methodology of spiritualistic fraud will find sufficient leads here to launch them well on their way.

Some books in this bibliography, such as Fodor's and Carrington's, take the view that though fraud exists, genuine psychic phenomena also exist. This is the view of William Rauscher, Allen Spraggett and, to a lesser extent, Lamar Keene.

Abbott, David P. *Behind the Scenes with the Medium.* Chicago: Open Court, 1907.

Anderson, George. "It Must Be Mind-Reading." Chicago: Ireland Magic, 1963.

————."You, Too, Can Read Minds." Chicago: Magic, 1968.

Annemann, Theodore. *Practical Mental Effects.* New York: Holden's Magic Shops, 1944. Methods of revealing unknown knowledge.

————."202 Methods of Forcing." Chicago: Magic, 1964.

Bach, Marcus. *The Will to Believe.* Englewood Cliffs, N.J.: Prentice-Hall. 1955 See Chapt. 10, "Do We Live After Death?" for account of a materialization seance with medium Fanchion Harwood.

Baggally, W. W. *Telepathy: Genuine and Fraudulent.* London: Methuen, 1920.

Barbanell, Maurice. "Seance Room Scoundrel." *Tomorrow Magazine 6,* No. 3, Summer 1958: p. 49. The story of the medium William Roy.

————.*This Is Spiritualism.* London: Herbert Jenkins, 1959

Bayless, Raymond. *Experiences of a Psychical Researcher.* New Hyde Park, N.Y.: University Books, 1972. See chapters 2, 27 and 28 on Spiritualism, Fakers, Magicians and Mediums.

Blackmore, Simon Augustine, S.J. *Spiritism Facts and Frauds.* New York: Benziger Brothers, Printers to the Holy Apostolic See, 1924. A tracing of spiritism from necromancy in ancient times from the viewpoint of the Catholic Church.

Blunsdon, Norman. *A Popular Dictionary of Spiritualism.* London: Arco Publications, 1961.

Bowers, Edwin F. *Spiritualism's Challenge.* New York: National Library Press, 1936. See Chapter 14, "Honest and Dishonest Mediums," and reports of the enigmatic mediumship of Frank Decker, with a report on his mail-sack escape and his association with Dunninger the magician. The checkered career of Eusapia Palladino confounds the writer of this book. She explains to a reporter, when asked if she had ever been caught cheating, "Many times I have been told so. You see, it is like this. Some people are at a table who expect tricks—in fact, they want them. I am in a trance. Nothing happens. They get impatient. They think of the tricks—nothing but tricks. They put their minds on the tricks, and I—and I automatically respond. But it is not often. They merely will me to do them. That is all."

Brown Slater. *The Heyday of Spiritualism.* New York: Hawthorn Books, 1970. Excellent history of the early days.

Cannell, J. C. *The Secrets of Houdini.* New York: Dover Publications, 1973.

"Carnival Torture Feats." Atlanta, Ga.: Pinchpenny Press, n.d. (mimeograph). How to perform physical feats of torture without getting hurt—everything from needle-jabbing and pulse control to putting your fingers in hot lead.

Carrington, Hereward. *Sideshow and Animal Tricks.* Kansas City: 1913; Atlantia, Ga.: Pinchpenny Press, 1973.

_____.*The Physical Phenomena of Spiritualism.* New York: American Universities, 1920. A critical book covering all phases of physical phenomena and explaining many methods still in use today.

_____.*Personal Experiences in Spiritualism.* London: T. Werner Laurie, n.d.

Christopher, Milbourne. "One Man Mental Magic." New York: Tannen Publications, 1952.

_____.*Mediums, Mystics and the Occult.* New York: Thomas Y. Crowell Company, 1975. A famous magician attempts to give the inside story on how to distinguish honest psychic research methods from the charlatans that prey upon the hopes and fears of the gullible. Well documented with many details.

_____.*Panorama of Magic.* New York: Dover Publications, 1962. See material on famous mentalists.

_____.*ESP, Seers, and Psychics.* New York: Thomas Y. Crowell, 1970. Although negative toward the reality of ESP and psychic phenomena, it does provide background material on specific psychic personalities but gives little credit to them or to reputable researchers. Fake methods are presented and postulated.

_____.*The Illustrated History of Magic.* New York: Thomas Y. Crowell, 1973. Material on mind-readers and mentalists.

Confessions of a Medium. London: Griffith, Farran, Okeden, and Welsh, 1882.

Confessions of a Medium. Columbus, O.: Nelson Enterprises, 1969 (mimeograph). Throws a "ruthless spotlight of truth on the grafters and frauds that infest the Spiritualistic movement and the psychic business."

_____. "The Nail Writer: Swami Gimmic, 24 Astounding Effects with the Mentalist's Miracle Gimmic, A Full Treatise on the Proper Handling of the Nail Writer. New York: Louis Tannen, n.d.

Corinda. *Thirteen Steps to Mentalism.* New York: Louis Tannen, 1968.

_____, and Read, Ralph W. (Ed.) *The Complete Guide to Billet-Switching.* New York: Louis Tannen, Inc., 1976. Booklet. This clever 46 page guide reminds you to look at the spectator when you switch a Billet—not your hands and when the spectator has written something to say "what you are thinking" NOT "what you have written." This work was compiled for entertainment purposes. It is important for the student and psychic researcher for learning the methods of billet switching so that public or private demonstrations by mediums, psychics and "mentalists" do not confuse and confound the sincere seeker.

Cox, William E. "Parapsychology and Magicians." *Parapsychology Review,* (May-June, 1974).

Curry, Paul. *Magician's Magic.* New York: Franklin Watts, 1965. See Chapter 10, "The Power of Thought."

Davenport, Reuben Briggs. *The Death Blow to Spiritualism.* New York: G. W. Dillingham, 1888. An attempt to write a true account of the origin of spiritualism, approved by Maggie and Kate Fox. Contains statements quoting them in respect to their fraudulent practices.

Dexter, Will. *This Is Magic:* Secrets of Conjurers' Craft. New York: Bell, 1948. See Chapter 14, "Is It Second Sight?"

Doyle, Arthur Conan, *The History of Spiritualism.* New York: George H. Doran Co., 1926. A sympathetic approach originally published at the author's own expense. Conan Doyle was interested in "phenomena for over 30 years." He says, "My one aim in life is that this great truth, the return and communion of the dead, shall be brought home to a material world which needs it so badly." Conan Doyle's credentials as a researcher were often in question especially when he attributed certain escapes of magician Houdini to dematerialization. It should be said that those who fault Conan Doyle as an investigator also pay tribute to his total integrity and unimpeachable character. The same cannot be said for Houdini in respect to his ego centered psychic investigations. Intriguing correspondence exists between the author of Sherlock Holmes and the Escapologist in the book *Houdini and Conan Doyle,* "The Story of a Strange Friendship" by Bernard M. L. Ernst and Hereward Carrington published by Albert and Charles Boni, Inc., New York, 1932.

Dunninger, Joseph. *Houdini's Spirit Expose: From Houdini's Own Manuscripts, Records, and Photographs, and Dunninger's Psychical Investigations.* New York: Experimenter, 1928.

_____.*Inside the Medium's Cabinet.* New York: David Kemp, 1935.

_____, as told to Gibson, Walter B. *Dunninger's Secrets.* Secaucus, N.J.: Lyle Stuart, Inc., 1974.

Edmund Scientific Company Catalog 761. Barrington, N.J.: 1976. Within the more than 4,500 items listed of a "scientific" nature are items suitable to the fake medium, such as black light paint, clear liquid that glows in the dark when applied to any surface, and a kit to transfer pictures and photos to cloth surfaces, plus other items from this supply house for industry, schools, and hobbyists.

Edmunds, Simeon. *Spiritualism: A Critical Survey.* London: Aquarian Press, 1966. Contains full account of exposed medium William Roy and his methods.

Evans, Henry Ridgely. *The Spirit World Unmasked.* Chicago: Laird and Lee, 1897.

_____. *Hours with the Ghosts.* Chicago: Laird and Lee, 1897. See methods used by the Davenport Brothers as originators of the Spirit Cabinet.

Fodor, Nandor. *Encyclopedia of Psychic Science.* New Hyde Park, N.Y.: University Books, 1966. See "Fraud."

_____. *The Haunted Mind.* New York: Helix Press—Garrett Publications, 1959. See chapter XVI—"Demon Lovers and Mediumship."

Frikell, Samri, *Spirit Mediums Exposed,* New York, New York Metropolitan Fiction, 1930. (Actually written by Fulton Oursler)

Fuller, Uriah. *Confessions of a Psychic,* The Secret Notebooks of Uriah Fuller, published by Karl Fulves, Box 433, Teaneck, New Jersey, 1975. A magician's view in booklet form of how fake psychics perform seemingly incredible paranormal feats. This is an attempt to speak for Uri Geller and to relate how he bends metal, reads sealed drawings and apports objects. It also hints at the possibility of Nina Kuglagina in Russia having magnets in her bra to move a compass and all the deceptive methods which may be employed in what the author believes is the "underground of deception." It makes the exaggerated claim that the only persons qualified to examine self-claimed psychics are magicians experienced in the "double think" or "lateral thinking" approach to their craft.

Gaines, Steven S. *Marjoe:* The Life of Marjoe Gortner. New York: Harper and Row, Publishers. 1973. The biography of a fake evangelist.

Gibson, Walter B. *The Bunco Book.* Holyoke, Mass.: Sidney H. Radner, 1946. Methods of confidence men and schemers from games of chance to short-changers.

_____, and Young, Morris N. *Houdini on Magic.* New York: Dover Publications, 1963.

Gresham, William Lindsay. *Nightmare Alley.* New York: Rinehart, 1946. A gripping novel of the rise and fall of a mind-reader.

Hall, Trevor H. *The Spiritualists.* New York: Helix Press, Garrett Publications, 1962.

Hardinge, Emma. *Modern American Spiritualism.* New Hyde Park, New York: University Books, 1970. A twenty-year record of Spiritualism in mid-nineteenth century America.

Hill, J. Arthur. *Spiritualism: Its History, Phenomena, and Doctrine.* New York: George Doran, 1919.

Houdini, Harry. *The Right Way to Do Wrong.* An Exposé of Successful Criminals. Boston, Mass.: Harry Houdini, 1906.

_____. "Houdini Exposes the Tricks Used by the Boston Medium "Margery." New York: Adams Press, circa 1924. Known as the famous "pink pamphlet."

_____. *A Magician Among the Spirits.* New York: Arno Press, 1972. This book details the adventures of Houdini the escapologist with spiritualists and mediums.

_____, and Dunninger, Joseph. *Magic and Mystery:* The Incredible Psychic Investigations of Houdini and Dunninger. New York: Tower Publications, 1968.

Hoy, David. "The Bold and Subtle Miracles of Dr. Faust." Chicago: Ireland Magic, 1963.

Hull, Burling. "The Last Word Blindfold Methods: 12 Sensational Blindfolds." Woodside, N.Y.: Burling Hull, 1946. Privately published.

————. *Thirty-Three Rope-Ties and Chain Releases.* New York: Stage Magic, 1947. All a fake medium needs to know about the art of rope-tying and release, including escape from a sack. Privately published.

————. *Encyclopedic Dictionary of Mentalism,* vol. 2. Calgary, Alberta, Canada: Micky Hades Enterprises, 1973. A gigantic collection of complete mentalism methods, secrets, instructions, and routines.

Jackson, Herbert G., Jr. *The Spirit Rappers.* New York: Doubleday, 1972. Letters, memoirs, court records, newspaper accounts, and journals are cited in this story of Kate and Maggie Fox, founders of the American Spiritualist Movement.

Kaye, Marvin. *The Handbook of Mental Magic.* New York: Stein and Day, publishers, 1975. An interesting book—pretentious and self important but interesting. The author calls himself Count Emkay the Miraculous and has written a pompous and self centered volume.

Kerr, Howard. *Mediums and Spirit Rappers, and Roaring Radicals.* Urbana: University of Illinois Press, 1972.

Knight, Marcus. *Spiritualism, Reincarnation, and Immortality.* London: Gerald Duckworth, 1950.

Kreskin. *The Amazing World of Kreskin.* New York: Random House, 1973. The author uses all the terms of parapsychology to lead the reader into accepting his mentalism tricks as something more. Allen Spraggett suggests that this book be retitled *The Not-So-Amazing World of Kreskin.*

Lawton, George. *The Drama of Life after Death:* A Study of the Spiritualist Religion. New York: Henry Holt, 1932.

Longridge, George. *Spiritualism and Christianity.* London: A. R. Mowbray, 1926.

Lustig, David J. *La Vellma's Vaudeville Budget.* For Magicians, mind-readers, mental telepathy, or silent thought-transference.

MacDougall, Curtis D. *Hoaxes.* New York: Dover Publications, Inc. 1958 A book about ingenious deceptions and fascinating frauds. Note Part I and II on incentives to believe and hoaxing in areas of the historical, religious, scientific, literary and governmental.

McHargue, Georgess. *Facts, Frauds, and Phantasms:* A Survey of the Spiritualist Movement. New York: Doubleday, 1972. A comprehensive and objective survey.

Medhurst, R. G. *Crookes and the Spirit World,* in association with K. M. Goldney and M. R. Barrington, New York, Taplinger Publisher Company, 1972. The investigations by Sr. William Crookes, OM, FRS in the field of psychical research.

Mental Catalogue. Box 476 Calgary, Alberta, Canada. Mickey Hades Enterprises.

Mental Magic and the Allied Arts. Catalog 28. Columbus, Ohio, 1966. (A former company catalog of the world's largest manufacturers of mental equipment.)

Menotti, Gian-Carlo. *The Medium.* New York: G. Schirmer, 1947. Opera libretto.

Morris, Bud. *Magic with Electronics.* Oakland, Calif.: privately published. Detailed methods of using microminiature electronics as aids in apparent mind-reading; author also supplies such items as subminiature wireless transmitters.

Mulholland, John. *Beware Familiar Spirits.* New York: Charles Scribner's Sons, 1938. Inside information on many of the methods used by such mediums as Anna Eva Fay and Henry Slade.

Nelson, Robert. *How to Read Sealed Messages.* Columbus, O.: Nelson Enterprises, 1961 (mimeograph).

_____. *Secret Methods of Private Readers!* Columbus, O.: Nelson Enterprises, 1964 (mimeograph). How to give psychic readings, switch billets and envelopes, and present private psychological or cold readings. It begins with the private reader's creed, "I like to see their eyes, mouth, and pocketbook open at the same time."

_____, and Moore, E. J. *Super Prediction Tricks.* Columbus, O.: Nelson Enterprises, n.d. (mimeograph). All you need to know to perform feats of prophecy, from predicting tomorrow's headline to a sentence selected from a book in the local library and then baked in a loaf of bread or frozen in a ton of ice.

O'Donnell, Elliot. *The Menace of Spiritualism.* New York: Frederick A. Stokes, 1920. This well-known writer of ghost books offers his views on spiritualism with the Old and New Testaments in mind, and has a chapter on the danger of fraud of all kinds.

O'Neill, Tom. "The Tragic Deceptions in Materializations." Southern Pines, N.C. *Psychic Observer.* July 10, Aug. 10, 1960.

Pages from a Medium's Notebook. Calgary, Alberta, Canada: Micky Hades Enterprises, 1971 (mimeograph). The ways and means of fake mediumship, by an anonymous author.

Pearsall, Ronald. *The Table-Rappers.* New York: St. Martin's Press, 1972. An excellent survey of Victorian Spiritualism. Contains many methods of fraudulent practices citing those caught cheating and how they did it.

Pidgeon, Charles (pseud.). *Revelations of a Spirit Medium.* Edited by Harry Price and Eric J. Dingwall, London: Kegan Paul, Trench, Trubner, 1922. Facsimile edition, with notes, bibliography, glossary, and index. This book was first published in 1891. Many of the methods described are dated, but the general opinion regarding "sitters" is still valid. Excellent glossary.

Podmore, Frank. *Mediums of the Nineteenth Century,* vols. 1 and 2. New Hyde Park, N.Y.: University Books, 1963. An indispensable account of great mediums and the problems of research by "the most formidable critic that Spiritualism has ever encountered."

Price, Harry. "Regurgitation and the Duncan Mediumship." London: *Bulletin of the National Laboratory of Psychical Research,* 1931. Believe it or not, the results showed that Mrs. Duncan could and did swallow and regurgitate so-called teleplasm, which was merely cheesecloth. Illustrations show, among other examples, how a piece of cheesecloth six feet long, thirty inches wide, and weighing 1½ ounces can be rolled into a small wad and placed in the mouth.

————. *Confessions of a Ghost Hunter.* New York: Causeway Books, 1974. Chapter 15, "Stage Telepathy and Vaudeville 'Phenomena,'" relates encounters and friendship with some of the great spellbinders of all time.

Proskauer, Julien J. *Spook Crooks!* New York: A. L. Burton, 1932.

Randi, The Amazing, *The Magic of Uri Geller.* New York: Ballantine Books. 1975. A purported exposé of Uri Geller. Funny in places but unreliable.

Rauscher, William V. "ESP and Mentalism." *Psychic.* Vol. V No. 4 (April, 1974): pg. 50

————, with Spraggett, Allen. *The Spiritual Frontier.* New York: Doubleday, Inc., 1975. See appendix on Houdini Code Mystery Solved.

Reilly, S. W. "Table-Lifting Methods Used by Fake Mediums." Chicago: Ireland Magic, 1957 (mimeograph).

Rinn, Joseph F. *Searchlight on Psychical Research.* London: Rider, 1954. A record of sixty years' work, with countless references to methods of fraud.

Roberts, Bechofer, C. E. *The Truth about Spiritualism.* London: Eyre and Spottiswood, 1932.

Robinson, William E. *Spirit Slate Writing and Kindred Phenomena.* New York: Munn and Company Scientific American Office, 1898. The author was associated with the famous magicians

Alexander, Herrmann, and Harry Kellar. He covers table-lifting, raps, ties, and slate tests, including séance spirit tricks.

Seybert Commission. *Preliminary Report of the Commission by University of Pennsylvania to Investigate Modern Spiritualism.* Philadelphia: J. B. Lippincott, 1887. Results are discouraging in this report, presented as "one of the most thorough investigations of the truth of Spiritualism ever attempted."

Somerlott, Robert. *"Here, Mr. Splitfoot."* New York: Viking Press, 1971.

Spence, Lewis. *An Encyclopedia of Occultism.* New Hyde Park, N.Y.: University Books, 1968. See "Fraud."

Spraggett, Allen. *The Unexplained.* New York: New American Library, 1967. See Chapter 6, "Frauds and Teasers."

————, with Rauscher, William V. *Arthur Ford: The Man Who Talked with the Dead.* New York: New American Library, 1973. See Chapter 6, "The Gospel of Spiritualism," Chapter 8, "Mentalists and Mediums," and Chapter 11, "The Bishop Pike Affair."

Stemman, Roy. *Spirits and Spirit Worlds.* New York: Doubleday and Co., 1976. A sympathetic though critical book lavishly illustrated with old and new photographs from the archives of Spiritualism.

Tanner, Don. "How to Do Headline Predictions." Chicago: Ireland Magic, 1957.

The Lambeth Conferences (1867–1948) Reports. London: S.P.C.K., 1948. See report on spiritualism.

Thurston, Herbert. *The Church and Spiritualism.* Milwaukee, Wis.: Bruce, 1933.

Tietze, Thomas R. *Margery.* New York: Harper and Row, 1973. An intriguing account of the medium Mina S. Crandon, known as Margery, and the perplexing events and personalities involved in her séances at the Crandon House on Lime Street in Boston, Massachusetts.

Whalen, William J. *Minority Religions in America.* New York: Alba House, Division of the Society of Saint Paul, 1972. "The Spiritualists," page 253, contains an account of a visit to Camp Chesterfield.

X, Dr. *On the Other Side of the Floodlights:* An Expose of Routines, Apparatus, and Deceptions Resorted to by Mediums, Clairvoyants, Fortune Tellers, and Crystal Gazers in Deluding the Public. Berlin, Wis.: Heaney Magic, 1922.

Zolotow, Maurice. *It Takes All Kinds.* New York: Random House, 1952. See chapter 2 on Dunninger.